Advent 2010

For Gail,

with love and prayers
on your Reception into the
Church 16ᵗʰ December 2010.

from your Sponsor,

Joanne

GW00570604

THE SAINTS
DAY BY DAY

*All you holy men and women,
pray for us.*

THE SAINTS DAY BY DAY

MINUTE MEDITATIONS FOR EVERY DAY TAKEN FROM THE WRITINGS OF THE SAINTS

•

Compiled and Edited
by
Marci Alborghetti

Illustrated

CATHOLIC BOOK PUBLISHING CORP.
New Jersey

CONTENTS

NIHIL OBSTAT: Rev. Msgr. James M. Cafone, M.A., S.T.D.
Censor Librorum

IMPRIMATUR: ✠ Most Rev. John J. Myers, J.C.D., D.D.
Archbishop of Newark

The Nihil Obstat and Imprimatur are official declarations that a book or a pamphlet is free of doctrinal or moral error. No implication is contained therein that those who have granted the Nihil Obstat and Imprimatur agree with the contents, opinions or statements expressed.

(T-185)

ISBN 978-0-89942-183-4

© 2009 Catholic Book Publishing Corp., N.J.

Printed in Korea

www.catholicbookpublishing.com

INTRODUCTION

THE Saints are images of God. They have put on Christ completely. To use the words of the early Christians of Smyrna: "We adore Christ because He is the Son of God; we love the Saints because they are disciples and imitators of our Lord."

In a St. Augustine of Hippo, we see Christ's art of instructing the people; in a St. Francis of Assisi, His overwhelming love for all creatures; in a St. Thomas Aquinas, His unparalleled wisdom.

In a St. Gertrude of Helfta, we glimpse our Lord's life of inner prayer; in a St. Catherine of Siena, His common sense; in a St. Thérèse of Lisieux, His acceptance of suffering for others.

In all the Saints we perceive our models, teachers, and intercessors. The Saints lived the Christian life to the full. In addition to their lives, their words are a gold mine of information on how to live the Christian life.

The minute meditations in this book are intended to impart some of that wisdom to the reader. Each day there is a short helpful citation from a Saint—in most cases the Saint who is honored by the Church on that day.

It is prefaced by a Bible text and followed by a prayer to the Saint—both related to the topic dealt with by the Saint.

The Saint whose name is printed at the top is the Saint honored by the Church on that day. The Saints' names followed with an asterisk are not found in the General Liturgical Calendar, but they are assigned to the date in question by the Church in her other documents, for example, the Martyrology (Book of Saints).

This book is intended to make available to Catholics the wisdom of the Saints in the most suitable way. In this respect, it puts into practice the words of the Second Vatican Council:

"When we look at the lives of those who have faithfully followed Christ, we are inspired with a new reason for seeking the City that is to come. At the same time, we are shown a safe path by which among the vicissitudes of this world and in keeping with our state in life we will be able to arrive at perfect union with Christ, that is, perfect holiness.

"God speaks to us in the Saints and gives a sign of His Kingdom. Since we have such a cloud of witnesses over us and such a witness to the truth of the Gospel, we are strongly drawn to that Kingdom" (*Constitution on the Church*, no. 50).

May He speak to every reader through this little testimonial to the Saints.

Mary, Mother of God +1st cent.   JAN. 1

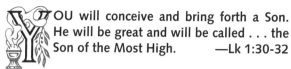

YOU will conceive and bring forth a Son. He will be great and will be called . . . the Son of the Most High.   —Lk 1:30-32

REFLECTION. How could anyone think that Mary has no power?

She deserves to be called Daughter of God the Father, Mother of God the Son, and Spouse of God the Holy Spirit!

—St. Bonaventure

PRAYER. *O Mary, teach me to imitate Your Divine Son in everything I do. In that way, I will be a true child of God.*

St. Basil +379   JAN. 2
St. Gregory Nazianzen +389

IT is mercy that I desire more than sacrifice; and knowledge of God rather than holocausts.   —Hos 6:6

REFLECTION. Those who love their neighbor love God, and God regards union with our neighbor as union with Him.   *—St. Basil*

God is worshiped more by mercy than by any single act. We must offer Him mercy for others rather than judgment of them.

—St. Gregory Nazianzen

PRAYER. *Sts. Basil and Gregory, help me to show my love for God by being kind to everyone I meet this day.*

JAN. 3 St. Genevieve +512*

 EEK first the Kingdom of God and His righteousness, and all these things will be given you. —Mt 6:33

REFLECTION. Those who give up the secular life are greater than all the honors and the kingdoms of this world. —*St. Cyprian*

PRAYER. *St. Genevieve, you dedicated your life to God. Help me to fulfill the duties of my state in life for the honor and glory of God.*

JAN. 4 St. Elizabeth Seton +1821

 HOEVER does the will of God is my brother and sister and mother. —Mk 3:35

REFLECTION. The first end I propose in our daily work is to do the will of God.

Secondly, to do it in the manner He wills; and thirdly, to do it because it is His will. —*St. Elizabeth Seton*

PRAYER. *St. Elizabeth, you were devoted to doing God's will in all things. Help me to discover what His will is for me and to carry it out faithfully each day.*

St. John Neumann +1860   **JAN. 5**

 NE and the same Spirit works all these things, distributing them individually to each person as He wills.

—1 Cor 12:11

REFLECTION. I have taken this burden [of the episcopacy] out of obedience.

I have labored with all my powers to fulfill the duties of my office, and with God's help, as I hope, not without fruit.

—*St. John Neumann*

PRAYER. *St. John, help me to be ever open to the inspirations of the Holy Spirit.*

Epiphany of the Lord   **JAN. 6**

 NTERING the house, they found the Child with Mary His Mother, and falling down they paid Him homage.   —Mt 2:11

REFLECTION. You were seeking God, and you have found that He is a being superior to all beings.

He is a being that which nothing better can be conceived.   —*St. Anselm*

PRAYER. *St. Anselm, intercede for me with the Lord of glory. Help me to find Jesus in my penance, good works, and prayer.*

JAN. 7   St. Raymond of Peñyafort +1275

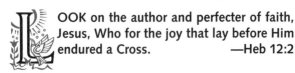

OOK on the author and perfecter of faith, Jesus, Who for the joy that lay before Him endured a Cross. —Heb 12:2

REFLECTION. Keep your eyes on Jesus, Who suffered in complete sinlessness.

As you drink the cup of the Lord Jesus, give thanks to the Lord, the giver of all blessings.

—*St. Raymond of Peñyafort*

PRAYER. *St. Raymond, you kept your eyes on Jesus throughout your long life. Grant that in all my words and actions I may do the same.*

JAN. 8   St. Severinus of Noricum +482*

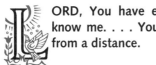

ORD, You have examined me and You know me. . . . You perceive my thoughts from a distance. —Ps 139:1-2

REFLECTION. God searches the hearts of all and understands all the imaginations of the mind.

Hope, therefore, by the help of constant prayer, that God may illumine the eyes of your heart. —*St. Severinus of Noricum*

PRAYER. *St. Severinus, you were favored with, among other things, the gift of prophecy. Pray that God will grant me the gift of true knowledge of the Faith.*

St. Adrian of Canterbury +710* JAN. 9

I ADVISE you to buy from me gold refined by fire.
—Rev 3:18

REFLECTION. Sacred Scripture is the Book of the Lord in which are contained the Lord's warnings and promises, gold refined by fire.

This gold is bought through diligent study and attentive meditation on the Scripture.
—*St. Albert the Great*

PRAYER. *St. Adrian, help me to meditate continually on the Word of God and put it into practice as you did.*

St. William +1209* JAN. 10

T HE love of Christ urges us forward. . . . [He] died for all, so that those who live might no longer live for themselves.
—2 Cor 5:14-15

REFLECTION. The Eucharist imparts to us habits of grace and virtue.

It also impels us to action in accord with the words of St. Paul: "The love of Christ impels us."
—*St. Thomas Aquinas*

PRAYER. *St. William, increase my love for the Eucharist that will be translated into good works.*

JAN. 11   St. Paulinus +804*

EASE your lying and speak the truth to each other.

—Eph 4:25

REFLECTION. We should have a deep love for the truth.

So much so, that all our words will have the value of oaths.   —*St. Paulinus*

PRAYER. *St. Paulinus, you loved truth and urged us to speak the truth. Help me to be truthful in all things and so imitate my Savior Who is the Truth itself.*

JAN. 12   St. Margaret Bourgeoys +1700*

OD is love, and those who abide in love abide in God.

—1 Jn 4:16

REFLECTION. Love your neighbor. Look at the source of your love of neighbor.

There you will see, as you may, God.

—*St. Margaret Bourgeoys*

PRAYER. *St. Margaret, you were suffused with love for neighbor. Help me to see Christ in others so that I will work and pray for their good.*

St. Hilary +367   JAN. 13

AKE to heart the words I am enjoining on you today. . . . Speak of them at home and abroad.   —Deut 6:4

REFLECTION. I am well aware, almighty God and Father, that in my life I owe You a most particular duty.

It is to make my every thought and word speak of You.   —*St. Hilary*

PRAYER. *St. Hilary, you dedicated your life to spreading the knowledge and love of God. Obtain for me the grace that others can encounter God through my words and deeds.*

St. Felix of Nola +260*   JAN. 14

HE Apostles rejoiced that they had been found worthy to suffer . . . for the Name of Jesus.   —Acts 5:41

REFLECTION. Let us not expect to find Love without suffering. Our nature is there; and it is not there for nothing.

But what treasures it enables us to acquire!
                    —*St. Theresa of Lisieux*

PRAYER. *St. Felix, help me to accept any suffering that comes my way and to offer it up in the Name of the Lord.*

JAN. 15   St. Ida +570*

 LL that is born of God overcomes the world. And this is the victory that overcomes the world: our faith. —Jn 5:4

REFLECTION. There are three things that God loves in a special way.

True faith in God with a pure heart, a simple life with a religious spirit, and an open hand inspired by charity. —*St. Ida*

PRAYER. *St. Ida, you served the Lord with great faith. Obtain for me a strong faith that can be translated into good works every passing day.*

JAN. 16   St. Honoratus of Arles +439*

 HANKS be to God Who has given us the victory through our Lord Jesus Christ. —1 Cor 15:57

REFLECTION. We owe great gratitude to Christ.

He dispels the terror of a death that lasts forever by the offer of a life that lasts forever. —*St. Honoratus of Arles*

PRAYER. *St. Honoratus, you urge us to be grateful for our salvation. Help me to show my gratitude to God every day both in word and in work.*

14

St. Anthony of Egypt +373   JAN. 17

 NO one who puts a hand to the plow but keeps looking back is fit for the Kingdom of God. —Lk 9:62

REFLECTION. Since we have set out and progressed in the path of virtue, we must proceed directly forward with all our might.

Let no one look back.

—*St. Anthony of Egypt*

PRAYER. *St. Anthony, pray that I may keep my eyes ever on Jesus and never backtrack in my spiritual life.*

Bl. Christina Ciccarelli +1543*   JAN. 18

 OUR Father in heaven. . . . Your will be done. —Mt 6:9-10

REFLECTION. The grand thing to be acquired by those who practice the habit of prayer is to conform their own will to the will of God.

In this consists the highest perfection.

—*St. Theresa of Avila*

PRAYER. *Blessed Christina, you embraced a spirit of obedience in imitation of the obedient Jesus. Help me to know what is God's will for me and to do it every day.*

E are confident that we have a right conscience, desiring to live honorably in every way.   —Heb 13:18

REFLECTION. By following a right conscience you do not incur sin.

Furthermore, you are immune from sin, no matter what your superiors may say to the contrary.   —*St. Thomas Aquinas*

PRAYER. *St. Wulstan, you refused to carry out a wicked command of William the Conqueror. Help me to follow a right conscience in all I say and do.*

JAN. 20   **Sts. Fabian and Sebastian** +250

LL who wish to live a good life in Christ Jesus will suffer persecution.
    —2 Tim 3:12

REFLECTION. "All" will suffer persecution; there is no exception.

How many there are today who are secret martyrs for Christ, giving testimony to Jesus as Lord!   —*St. Ambrose*

PRAYER. *Sts. Fabian and Sebastian, you gave your lives for the Lord. Help me to accept all the crosses of each day as a kind of spiritual martyrdom for Christ.*

St Agnes +350   JAN. 21

 EXHORT you as strangers and pilgrims to abstain from carnal desires, which war against the soul.   — 1 Pet 2:11

REFLECTION. Today is the birthday of a virgin; let us imitate her purity.

It is the birthday of a martyr; let us offer ourselves in sacrifice.   *—St Ambrose*

PRAYER. *St. Agnes, you gave up your life to safeguard your purity. Pray that I too may be willing to give up anything that imperils my purity.*

St. Vincent of Saragossa +304   JAN. 22

N the world, you will have affliction. But take courage, I have overcome the world.   —Jn 16:33

REFLECTION. When we feel too bold, let us remember our feebleness.

When we feel too weak, let us remember Christ's strength.   *—St. Thomas More*

PRAYER. *St. Vincent, help me to put all my trust in my Redeemer so that I may overcome all adversity.*

JAN. 23   St. Ildefonsus +667*

BEHOLD as the eyes of servants are on the hands of their masters . . . so are our eyes fixed on the Lord our God till he shows us mercy. —Ps 123:2

REFLECTION. I want to be a devoted servant of the Heavenly Father.

Therefore, I faithfully desire to be the servant of the Mother. *—St. Ildefonsus*

PRAYER. *St. Ildefonsus, you were devoted to God and to Mary. Obtain for me true devotion to the Mother of God so that I may go to Jesus through Mary.*

JAN. 24   St. Francis de Sales +1622

LORD, . . . keep my life, for I am devoted to You; save Your servant who trusts in You. —Ps 6:2

REFLECTION. True devotion not only does no harm to any vocation or occupation but also embellishes and enhances it.

Everyone's vocation becomes more agreeable when united with devotion.

—St. Francis de Sales

PRAYER. *St. Francis, you taught many how to attain the devout life. Enable me to practice true devotion to God every day of my life.*

Conversion of St. Paul

JAN. 25

THE Gospel that I preach is not from human hands. I received it by revelation of Jesus Christ. —Gal 1:11-12

REFLECTION. We must listen to the Gospel as if the Lord Himself were present and speaking to us.

The very prayers that fell from the lips of Christ were written down, safeguarded, and handed down to us. —*St. Augustine*

PRAYER. *St. Paul, help me to find Christ in the Gospel and bear witness to Him every day.*

Sts. Timothy and Titus +96-97

JAN. 26

PURSUE justice, godliness, faith, charity, patience, mildness. Fight the good fight of the faith. —1 Tim 6:11-12

REFLECTION. Virtue does not consist in starting to do good but in carrying it out to the end.

The reward is promised not to those who begin well but to those who end well.

—*St. Isidore*

PRAYER. *Sts. Timothy and Titus, you proclaimed the Gospel with courage and wisdom. Pray that I may lead a good life and reach heaven, my true home.*

JAN. 27 St. Angela Merici +1540

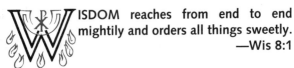

WISDOM reaches from end to end mightily and orders all things sweetly.
—Wis 8:1

REFLECTION. Take care that what you command may never be done through force.

For God has given free will to everyone, and therefore He forces no one but only indicates, calls, persuades. —*St. Angela Merici*

PRAYER. *St. Angela, in your quiet way you revolutionized the role of women in education. Teach me how to use persuasion rather than force in my dealings with others.*

JAN. 28 St. Thomas Aquinas +1274

THIS is the victory that overcomes the world, our faith.
—Ps 6:2

REFLECTION. The virtue of faith is in no way an inconvenience or a burden for us.

Rather, it is an immense benefit, beginning eternal life in us even here below.
—*St. Thomas Aquinas*

PRAYER. *St. Thomas, you wrote great works about God that enlightened our faith. Help me to grow in faith every day and so increase the Divine Life in us.*

20

St. Gildas +570*   JAN. 29

IF you turn away from doing your own will . . .
you shall be delighted in the Lord.
                                        —Isa 58:13-14

REFLECTION. We must beware of preferring
fasting to charity, our own ideas to peace-
ableness, privacy to praying with others in
church.

In short, we must beware of preferring
human beings to God.   —*St. Gildas*

PRAYER. *St. Gildas, you always put God first
in all the circumstances of your life. Teach me
how to overcome my own preferences and to
do what God wills.*

St. Bathildis +680*   JAN. 30

YOU are anxious and troubled about many
things. Yet only one thing is necessary.
                                        —Lk 10:42

REFLECTION. We must ransom the time by sac-
rificing present interests for those of eternity.

In this way, we will gain heaven with
earthly coin.   —*St. Augustine*

PRAYER. *St. Bathildis, you gave up wealth
and power for closeness to God. Teach me to
use the things of earth only to gain heaven.*

FEB.1 St. Bridgid (Bride) of Ireland +c. 525*

RAISE the name of the Lord; offer Him praise, you servants of the Lord, you who minister in the house of the Lord.

—Ps 135:1-2

REFLECTION. My storehouse shall be one of bright testimony, a storehouse that my King shall bless, a storehouse overflowing with abundance.

The Son of Mary, Who is my beloved One, will bless my storehouse. His is the glory of the whole universe.   —St. Bridgid

PRAYER. *St. Bridgid, as the legend says of you, help me to "satisfy the poor, and expel every hardship."*

FEB.2   The Presentation of the Lord

OW there was a man in Jerusalem whose name was Simeon; this man was righteous and devout.   —Lk 2:25

REFLECTION. Let us make haste to meet Christ. Everyone should be ready to join in the procession and to bear a light.

My brothers and sisters, let all of us, be enlightened and made radiant by this light.

—St. Sophronius

PRAYER. *Jesus, I rejoice with Simeon and the whole world, welcoming You into my life with praise and gratitude.*

St. Blase +320   **FEB.3**

 F you abide in Me and My words abide in you, ask for whatever you wish and it will be done for you. —Jn 15:7

REFLECTION. Through the merits and intercession of St. Blase, Bishop and Martyr, may God deliver you from ailments of the throat and from every other evil.

In the name of the Father, and of the Son, and of the Holy Spirit. Amen.

—*Blessing of St. Blase*

PRAYER. *St. Blase, intercede for me and those I love so that we may be in good health and spirits.*

St. John de Britto +1693*   **FEB.4**

 ESUS answered (Pilate), "You would have no power over Me unless it had been given you from above." —Jn 19:11

REFLECTION. My friend, I have done what I should do, I have prayed to God. Now do your part. Carry out the order you have received.

—*St. John, to his executioner*

PRAYER. *St. John, you returned to the place of your persecution to do God's work. I pray for all who are in danger as they serve God.*

St. Agatha +c. 251

 UT in my righteousness I will see Your face; when I awaken, I will be blessed by beholding You. —Ps 17:15

REFLECTION. Lord, my Creator, You have taken care of me since I was in the cradle. You have delivered me from the love of the world and granted me patience to suffer.

Now receive my spirit. —St. Agatha

PRAYER. *St. Agatha, miracles were attributed to you after you suffered martyrdom. Help me to put my suffering to good use in prayer and service.*

FEB. 6 **Sts. Paul Miki and Companions** +1597

 HE fruit of the Spirit is love, joy, peace, patience, kindness, generosity, faithfulness, gentleness, and self-control. —Gal 5:22-23

REFLECTION. The only reason for me being killed is that I have taught the doctrine of Christ. I thank God I die for this reason.

Please believe me. I say to you all once again: Ask Christ to help you to be happy. —St. Paul Miki

PRAYER. *Lord Jesus, grant me the happiness and fulfillment that is only found in You.*

St. Richard of Lucca +c. 720*   **FEB. 7**

AY our God and Father Himself and our Lord Jesus prepare the way to you.
—1 Thes 3:11

REFLECTION. God is the beginning, the middle and the end of every good thing.

But the good cannot become active or be believed in other than through Jesus Christ and the Holy Spirit.   —*St. Mark the Ascetic*

PRAYER. *St. Richard, you are recognized as the father of three children who became Saints. Help me to encourage my family members to be faithful.*

St. Jerome Emiliani +1537   **FEB. 8**

HE Father of orphans and the defender of widows is God in His holy dwelling. God gives a home to the forsaken.
—Ps 68:6-7

REFLECTION. I urge you to persevere in your love for Christ, and your faithfulness to the law of Christ.

Our goal is God, the Source of all that is good.   —*St. Jerome*

PRAYER. *St. Jerome, patron of orphans, help me to care for the poor as you did.*

FEB. 9 St. Miguel Cordero +1910*

 HOM do I have in heaven except You? And besides You there is nothing else I desire on earth. —Ps 73:25

REFLECTION. The heart is rich when it is content, and the heart is always content when its desires are focused on God.

Nothing can bring one greater happiness than doing God's will. —St. Miguel

PRAYER. *St. Miguel you brought many young people to God. Let me "fix my desires" on God.*

FEB. 10 St. Scholastica +c. 547

 ETER did not realize that the intervention of the angel was real, thinking that he was seeing a vision. —Acts 12:9

REFLECTION. I appealed to you and you would not listen to me. So I turned to my God and He heard my prayer.

Leave now if you can.

—St. Scholastica to her brother, St. Benedict, after God sent a storm to prevent him from leaving her.

PRAYER. *St. Scholastica, keep me close to my family and friends in the Lord.*

Our Lady of Lourdes 1858 **FEB. 11**

GREAT sign appeared in heaven: a woman clothed with the sun, with the moon beneath her feet, and a crown of twelve stars on her head. —Rev 12:1

REFLECTION. For those who believe in God, no explanation is necessary.

For those who do not believe, no explanation is possible. —*Song of Bernadette*

PRAYER. *Mary, Our Lady of Lourdes, open my eyes to the message and miracles of your Son that are given to me every day and in so many ways.*

Bl. Humbeline +1163* **FEB. 12**

HE One Who is coming after me is more powerful than I am. I am not worthy to carry His sandals. —Mt 3:11

REFLECTION. Selfish ambition is the mother of hypocrisy and prefers to hide in corners and dark places. It cannot withstand the light of day.

Such ambition is an unclean vice wallowing in the depths, staying hidden, but always with an eye to advancement. —*St. Bernard*

PRAYER. *Bl. Humbeline, let me live humbly as you did in following your brother, Bernard, into service.*

27

FEB. 13   Bl. Jordan of Saxony +1237*

ESUS answered, "Where I am going, you cannot follow Me now, but you will follow Me later."   —Jn 13:36

REFLECTION. If any one of you be sad for a time . . . so that the torrent of devoted love seems absent . . . realize the Lord's way.

Sometimes He will draw away from you so that you may seek Him with greater zeal, and . . . find Him with greater joy.   —Bl. Jordan

PRAYER. *Bl. Jordan, teach me to always seek the Lord with all my heart, soul, and mind.*

FEB. 14   St. Cyril +869 and St. Methodius +885

OU established the earth on its foundations . . . You covered the deep like a cloak; the waters rose above the mountains.   —Ps 104:5-6

REFLECTION. I began to praise the Creator as I saw the stability of the earth and variety of living creatures in it.

Nothing is eternally co-existent with God except God Himself but . . . whatever exists has its origin in Him.   —St. Methodius

PRAYER. *Sts. Cyril and Methodius, with you I praise God's creation and strive to care for it well.*

St. Claude de la Colombiere +1682* FEB. 15

 ND I will ask the Father, and He will give you another Advocate to be with you forever. —Jn 14:16

REFLECTION. You are my true friend, my only friend, dearest Jesus. You take my misfortunes upon Yourself and You change them into blessings.

With the greatest kindness You listen to me when I tell You my troubles. —*St. Claude*

PRAYER. *St. Claude, counselor and converter of saints and royalty, let me turn to Jesus for wisdom and comfort.*

St. Maruthas +c. 416* FEB. 16

 OU shook the earth and split it apart; repair its cracks, for it continues to shake. —Ps 60:4

REFLECTION. Christ says, "Where two or three are gathered together in My name, there am I in the midst of them."

Imagine when an entire congregation is gathered in the name of the Lord . . . make yourselves worthy so that Christ will be in your midst. —*St. Ambrose*

PRAYER. *St. Maruthas, father of the Syrian Church, intercede for and protect the Church in the Middle East.*

FEB. 17   **Seven Founders of the Order**
                 of Servites +Thirteenth Century

 IVE my greetings to every one of the saints in Christ Jesus.   —Phil 4:21

REFLECTION.   Let all religious teach the good news of Christ by the integrity of their faith.

With the powerful aid of that most loving Virgin Mary, God's Mother, religious communities will experience a daily growth.

—*Decree on the Renewal of Religious Life*

PRAYER.   *Seven Founders, servants of Jesus and Mary, keep me from distractions when serving the Lord.*

FEB. 18   **St. Theotonius** +c. 1162*

 MEN, amen, I say to you, whoever believes has eternal life.

—Jn 6:47

REFLECTION.   Death, you hide from those who long for you, and stay close to those who flee from you.

I am certain it would be impossible to find any greater joy than that of a soul in purgatory, except . . . of the blessed in paradise.

—*St. Catherine of Genoa*

PRAYER.   *St. Theotonius, I join you in praying for the souls in purgatory.*

Bl. Conrad of Piacenza +1351*   FEB. 19

 I AM at the point of exhaustion, and my grief is with me constantly. I acknowledge my iniquity, and I sincerely grieve for my sin.
—Ps 38:18-19

REFLECTION. For the living, repentance is never too late.

The approach to God's mercy is open.
—*St. Cyprian*

PRAYER. *Bl. Conrad, you repented of your sin, thus saving the life of an innocent man and your own. Teach me the joy of repentance and atonement.*

St. Eucherius +c. 738*   FEB. 20

 A ND whoever receives one such child in My name receives Me. —Mt 18:5

REFLECTION. Lord, remember the bitter death that You endured for me, a poor sinner, and give me the grace to continue the good that I have begun.

O my Mercy, do not forget me. O my Refuge, do not leave me. —*Bl. Henry Suso*

PRAYER. *St. Eucherius, you remained meek even when dealing with the powerful. Teach me to be meek in pursuing Jesus' cause.*

31

St. Peter Damian +1072

HOW beautiful are the feet of those who proclaim the good news!

—Isa 52:7

REFLECTION.　Lord, have mercy, on those who pray to You for me, and on all who have asked me to pray for them.

Give them the spirit of fruitful penance to discipline all vices and make them abundant in all Your virtues.　　　*—St. Peter Damian*

PRAYER.　*St. Peter, you celebrated the power of prayer. Help me remember that prayer is my path to God.*

FEB. 22　Chair of St. Peter the Apostle

BLESSED be the God and Father of our Lord Jesus Christ, Who in His great mercy gave us a new birth . . . through the resurrection of Jesus Christ from the dead. **—1 Pet 1:3**

REFLECTION.　Out of the whole world one man, Peter, is chosen to rule over all the nations and to be above all the apostles and all the fathers of the Church.　　　*—St. Leo the Great*

PRAYER.　*St. Peter, show today's secular and clerical leaders the way to rule in the Lord and for the Lord.*

St. Polycarp +c. 155   FEB. 23

 O one can have greater love than to lay down his life for his friends.

—Jn 15:13

REFLECTION. Be strong and seek to follow the Lord's example, steadfast in your faith, loving the community as you love each other.

United in truth, be as gentle as the Lord in your dealings with one another, and look down on no one. —*St. Polycarp*

PRAYER. *St. Polycarp, let me turn to the words of your teacher, John the Evangelist, to strengthen my own faith.*

Bl. Josepha Naval Girbes +1893*   FEB. 24

 AY there be no breach in our walls, no going into exile, no cries of distress in our streets. —Ps 144:14

REFLECTION. O my God, I behold the mystery of the infinite abyss of Your mercy ever before me.

Thanks be to You for preserving my life until this day and for granting me repentance for my sins. —*St. Ignatius of Loyola*

PRAYER. *Bl. Josepha, you contemplated God's mysteries from your home. May I seek God from wherever I am.*

FEB. 25   Bl. Sebastian of Aparicio +1600*

O and sell what you own, and give to the poor, and you will have treasure in heaven.   —Mk 10:21

REFLECTION.   In the midst of worldly amusements, He shot at me flaming arrows that pierced and burned up my heart.

I felt that I was bound and pulled by ropes, so strongly that in the end I was forced to follow Him.   —*St. Margaret Mary Alocoque*

PRAYER.   *Bl. Sebastian, you remind me that it is never too late to turn my possessions and myself over to God.*

FEB. 26   St. Porphyrius +421*

OW that we have been justified by Christ's blood, how much more certainly will we be saved through Him from divine retribution.   —Rom 5:9

REFLECTION.   Let the worldly indulge themselves, for the madness cannot endure and will pass like a shadow.

But for those who are deeply bound to Christ, why should we be dismayed?
—*St. Peter Canisius*

PRAYER.   *St. Porphyrius, healed by a miracle, let me seek healing with a hopeful heart.*

St. Gabriel of Our Lady
of Sorrows +1862*

FEB. 27

TAKE care that you do not despise one of these little ones, for . . . their angels in heaven gaze continually on the face of My heavenly Father. —Mt 18:10

REFLECTION. Through God's Divine Mercy I would rather be the least among the Passionists than be the son of the king and heir to the kingdom.

I want to do God's holy will, not my own.

—*St. Gabriel*

PRAYER. *St. Gabriel, patron of youth, intercede for youngsters and protect them in these difficult, confusing times.*

———

Bl. Daniel Brottier +1936*

FEB. 28

WAIT for and speed the coming of the Day of God on which the heavens will be set ablaze. —2 Pet 3:12

REFLECTION. With all God's beautiful creation before me, my restless soul longs to enjoy its liberty and rest beyond its bounds.

When the Father calls His child, how readily He will be heard. —*St. Elizabeth Seton*

PRAYER. *Bl. Daniel, your obedience in your wide-ranging work shows me the need to follow whenever my Father calls.*

FEB. 29 — St. Oswald +992*

HOSE who have come to believe in God will be determined to devote themselves to good works. —Tit 3:8

REFLECTION. It is no small thing that God is going to give to those who yearn for Him; only hard work will get them to the goal.

God is going to give them more than what He has made; He is going to give Himself.

—*St. Augustine*

PRAYER. *St. Oswald, your zeal for reform reminds me that we must work and pray hard to reach God.*

MAR. 1 — St. David +c. 601*

ASTEN your belts for service and have your lamps lit. Be like servants who are waiting for their master to return so that they may open the door. —Lk 12:35-36

REFLECTION. Be joyful and keep the faith.

Do those little things you have seen and heard from me.

—*St. David's last words to his monks*

PRAYER. *St. David, your serene asceticism and abandonment of all your wealth is a good reminder to us that all we need is God.*

Bl. Angela of the Cross
Guerrero +1932*

 O not be concerned about your life and what you will . . . eat, or . . . what you will wear. —Lk 12:22

REFLECTION. What do . . . riches afford us in this world when they do not affect our birth or impede our dying?

We come into this world naked, we leave with nothing, we are buried without our inheritance. —*St. Ambrose*

PRAYER. *Bl. Angela, your decision to serve and live with the poor leads me to examine my own attachment to wealth and comfort.*

St. Katharine Drexel +1955

 LTHOUGH I am despised and unimportant, I do not forget Your commands. —Ps 119:141

REFLECTION. The patient and humble endurance of our crosses—whatever they may be—is the greatest work we have to do.

How far I am at 84 from being an image of Jesus in His sacred life on earth! —*St. Katharine*

PRAYER. *St. Katharine your enormous personal and financial commitment to minorities teaches me to help them today.*

MAR. 4   St. Casimir +1484

 UT I say to you: offer no resistance to someone who is wicked.

—Mt 5:39

REFLECTION. Anger is tempered and transformed into benevolence only through courage and mercy; for these destroy the enemies that attack the soul—first, the enemies outside and then, those within. —*St. Gregory of Sinai*

PRAYER. *St. Casimir, your youthful stand against war teaches me that we can all seek and stand for peace in our time.*

MAR. 5   St. Virgil +c. 618*

 HE hour is coming . . . when the true worshipers will worship the Father in Spirit and truth. —Jn 4:23

REFLECTION. O Lord, blend our humanity with Your divinity, Your greatness with our humility, that we may make an acceptable offering, which You made for the salvation of humankind. —*St. Gregory the Great*

PRAYER. *St. Virgil, your commitment to creating places of worship makes me grateful for the many places where I can worship God.*

St. Chrodegang +766*   MAR. 6

 ORD . . . grant that Your servants may proclaim Your word with all boldness.

—Acts 4:29

REFLECTION. Though Creator of all things, He chose to become human.

Yet this was an act of compassion, not the loss of omnipotence.

So He, Who in His divine nature created man, became in the nature of a servant, human Himself. —*St. Leo the Great*

PRAYER. *St. Chrodegang, your pursuit of social justice teaches me to help the disenfranchised.*

St. Perpetua and   MAR. 7
St. Felicity +203

 LIE prostrate in the midst of lions who are hungrily seeking human prey.

—Ps 57:5

REFLECTION. Do you see this vessel? Can you call it by any other name than what it is?

So then I cannot call myself by any other name than what I am—a Christian. —*St. Perpetua*

PRAYER. *Sts. Perpetua and Felicity, you gave up your newborns and your lives to proclaim Christ. I ask for a fraction of your courage.*

MAR. 8 St. John of God +1550

WHATEVER you did for one of the least of these brethren of Mine, you did for Me. —Mt 25:40

REFLECTION. The Son of Man died for sinners, and we are bound to seek their conversion.

I am unfaithful to my call if I neglect this, but I admit that I know of no sinner in my hospital except for myself. —*St. John*

PRAYER. *St. John, your devotion to caring for the impoverished sick led some to question your morality. May I care only for Jesus' opinion.*

MAR. 9 St. Frances of Rome +1440

JESUS approached her, grasped her by the hand, and helped her up. Then the fever left her, and she began to serve them. —Mk 1:31

REFLECTION. It is most laudable in a married woman to be devout, but she must never forget her duties as a wife.

Sometimes she must leave God at the altar to find Him in her housework. —*St. Frances*

PRAYER. *St. Frances, help me to balance my life so that I may seek and find God everywhere, in everything.*

St. Macarius +c. 325*   **MAR. 10**

OD has made this Jesus Whom you crucified both Lord and Christ.   —Acts 2:36

REFLECTION.   Lord Jesus Christ, Son of the
living God, have mercy on me, a sinner.

                            —*St. Macarius*

   Teach me from Your cross, Jesus, the feelings of love and forbearance that I should
have for my neighbor.   —*St. Louise de Marillac*

PRAYER.   *St. Macarius, you miraculously dis-
covered the true Cross in Jerusalem. May the
Cross be a symbol of all Jesus died for and
calls us to be.*

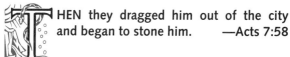

St. Eulogius +859*   **MAR. 11**

HEN they dragged him out of the city
and began to stone him.   —Acts 7:58

REFLECTION.   Remember Your mercies of old.

   Turn Your compassionate eyes upon the
vineyard planted by Your own right hand, and
watered by the tears of the Apostles and by
the precious blood of martyrs.

                 —*St. Clement Mary Hofbauer*

PRAYER.   *St. Eulogius, your support of saints
and martyrs led to your own martyrdom. I
pray for today's saints and martyrs.*

MAR. 12   St. Seraphina +1253*

 HEN Jesus said to Thomas, "Do not doubt any longer, but believe."

—Jn 20:27

REFLECTION.   We have reason for great joy: "Blessed are those who have not seen and have believed."

This is a particular reference to ourselves. We hold in our hearts One we have not seen in the flesh.   —*St. Gregory the Great*

PRAYER.   *St. Seraphina, in your suffering you prayed to St. Gregory. May I find relief in the words of the saints.*

MAR. 13   St. Leander of Seville +c. 600*

 HEN the Spirit of truth comes . . . He will take what is Mine . . . Everything that the Father has is Mine.

—Jn 15:13,14,15

REFLECTION.   We believe that the Father, and the Son, and the Holy Spirit are consubstantial, three (persons), one essence, one divinity.

That is the one, true faith handed down by the Fathers, and is prophetic, evangelical, and apostolic.   —*St. Epiphanius*

PRAYER.   *St. Leander, your promotion of the Nicene Creed reminds me of the beauty and importance of this prayer.*

St. Mathilda +968*   MAR. 14

 HEY said, "Behold, Your mother and Your brethren . . ." Jesus replied, "Who are My mother and My brethren."

—Mk 3:32, 33

REFLECTION. For me the greatest happiness in life is to be free from the cares and formalities of what is called the world.

My world is my family.   —*St. Elizabeth Seton*

PRAYER. *St. Mathilda, queen and mother, your devotion to your family inspires me to attend to the souls closest to mine.*

———————

St. Louise de Marillac +1660*   MAR. 15

 ND forgive us our debts as we forgive our debtors.

—Mt 6:12

REFLECTION. What were Your words during the torments of Your bitter passion? "Father, forgive them, they know not what they do!"

Jesus, our infinite Goodness . . . what a lesson You teach us . . . we should forgive those who have hurt us!   —*St. Louise*

PRAYER. *St. Louise, lead me to show forgiveness, patience, and kindness to everyone I meet.*

MAR. 16   St. Eusebia +c. 680*

E spoke to them from the pillar of the cloud; they obeyed His decrees and the law He gave them. —Ps 99:7

REFLECTION. I pledge obedience to You because Your Fatherly charity delights me, Your loving kindness and gentleness attract me.

By observing Your will, I bind myself to You. —*St. Gertrude the Great*

PRAYER. *St. Eusebia, obedience to your grandmother, St. Gertrude, allowed your gifts to shine. Teach me obedience.*

———————

MAR. 17   St. Patrick +461

F the earthly tent in which we live is destroyed, we have a dwelling prepared for us by God. —2 Cor 5:1

REFLECTION. I rise today
Through a mighty strength, the invocation of the Trinity,
Through belief in the threeness,
Through confession of the oneness
Of the Creator of Creation.

I rise today
through God's strength to pilot me.—*St. Patrick*

PRAYER. *St. Patrick, help me to follow God, filled with faith, as you did.*

St. Cyril of Jerusalem +386   **MAR. 18**

 HIS cup is the new covenant in My blood, which will be poured out for you.
—Lk 22:20

REFLECTION. Since Jesus Himself has said . . . of the bread, "This is My Body," who dares to doubt it?

And since He has declared . . . , "This is My Blood," who shall ever hesitate to say this is not His Blood? —*St. Cyril*

PRAYER. *St. Cyril, in your devotion to the Body and Blood of Jesus, increase my yearning for the Holy Eucharist.*

———————

St. Joseph +First Century   **MAR. 19**

 OSEPH was a just man and did not wish to expose her to the ordeal of public disgrace.
—Mt 1:19

REFLECTION. Joseph . . . was chosen by God to be the trustworthy guardian and protector of the Father's greatest treasures, namely, His divine Son and Mary.

Joseph was completely faithful until at last God called him. —*St. Bernardine of Siena*

PRAYER. *St. Joseph, be the perfect model for all husbands, fathers, priests, and leaders in our troubled world.*

MAR. 20   St. Cuthbert +687*

 FTER withdrawing from them about a stone's throw, He knelt down and prayed. —Lk 22:41

REFLECTION. Cuthbert used to go forth from his cell . . . and minister to them.

He shut himself up in the hermitage to live a solitary life of fasting, prayers, and vigils.

—St. Bede the Venerable.

PRAYER. *St. Cuthbert, help me to focus my whole being on God through solitude, fasting, and prayer.*

MAR. 21   St. Nicholas of Flue +1487*

 N God alone be at rest, O my soul; it is from Him that my hope comes.

—Ps 62:6

REFLECTION. Learn to dwell attentively in loving waiting upon God in silence.

Contemplation is a silent, peaceful, and loving infusion of God that will set the soul on fire with the Spirit of love.

—St. John of the Cross

PRAYER. *St. Nicholas, peacemaker, give me the grace to bring peace to others through my own inner peace.*

St. Lea +c. 383*   MAR. 22

 God, You have taught me from my youth, and to this day I proclaim Your marvelous works.   —Ps 71:17

REFLECTION. Who will honor Lea as she deserves?

Lea dwelt in a corner with a few pieces of furniture; she spent her nights in prayer and instructed her companions through her example rather than through . . . speeches.

—St. Jerome

PRAYER. *St. Lea, help me to bring myself and —through my example—others to greater contemplation of the Lord.*

St. Toribio de Mogrovejo +1606   MAR. 23

 VERYONE who is of the truth listens to My voice.   —Jn 18:37b

REFLECTION. Christ said, "I am the truth;" He did not say, "I am the custom."   —St. Toribio

There is but one baptism to us according to both the Lord's Gospel and according to the Apostle's letter.   —Tertullian

PRAYER. *St. Toribio, you used Tertullian's words to encourage fidelity to Christ. May I do not what is convenient as a Christian, but what is necessary.*

MAR. 24 St. Catherine of Sweden +1381*

 HAVE given you an example. What I have done for you, you should also do.

—Jn 13:15

REFLECTION. Jesus, You foretold Your death and at the Last Supper You marvelously consecrated bread which became Your precious Body. By washing the Apostles' feet with Your holy hands, You gave us a supreme example of humility. —St. Bridget

PRAYER. *St. Catherine, just as you followed your mother, St. Bridget, in humility and service, may I follow you.*

MAR. 25 The Annunciation of the Lord

 EHOLD the handmaid of the Lord; be it done to me according to Thy word.

—Lk 1:38

REFLECTION. Virgin, you have heard what will happen and how it will happen.

You have two reasons for astonishment and rejoicing. Rejoice, O Daughter of Sion, and be exceedingly glad, Daughter of Jerusalem.

—St. Bernard of Clairvaux

PRAYER. *Mary, daughter of God and mother of us all, I rejoice in you and thank you!*

St. Ludger +809*   MAR. 26

HO is greater, the one at table, or the one who serves? And yet I am in your midst as One Who serves.

—Lk 22:27

REFLECTION. Although He rose from the dead and can die no more, He lives in Himself immortal and incorruptible and is again immolated for us in the mystery of the Holy Sacrifice.

His Flesh is distributed among the people for our salvation.   —*St. Gregory*

PRAYER. *St. Ludger, student of St. Gregory, lend me your steadfast determination to serve Christ.*

Bl. Peregrine of Falerone +1232*   MAR. 27

EACH me Your ways, O Lord, so that I may walk in Your truth.

—Ps 86:11

REFLECTION. Make me an instrument of Your peace. Where there is hatred, let me sow love;
Where there is injury, pardon;
Where there is doubt, faith;
Where there is despair, hope;
Where there is darkness, light;
Where there is sadness, joy.   —*St. Francis of Assisi*

PRAYER. *Bl. Peregrine, after hearing St. Francis preach, you spent your life in humble service. Open my ears to blessed words.*

MAR. 28   St. Stephen Harding +1134*

 ESUS asked, "Who do you say that I am?" Peter answered, "You are the Christ."
—Mk 8:29

REFLECTION. We ask you that you never presume to change or disparage the integrity of the Holy Rule which you know has been written and established by us . . . with hard work, but rather living as lovers, imitators, and defenders of our holy Father.   —St. Stephen

PRAYER. *St. Stephen, help me to be disciplined and single-minded in doing God's work.*

MAR. 29   St. Mark +364*

 ESUS made it clear that He must go to Jerusalem and endure great suffering . . . and be put to death and be raised.
—Mt 16:21

REFLECTION. Jesus said that we must be slain and detested for His name's sake and that many prophets and false Christs would go forth in His name and would lead many astray.

And this is the case.   —St. Justin Martyr

PRAYER. *St. Mark, your courage in the face of persecution won you converts. Let me be converted to discipleship by the suffering of others.*

St. John Climacus +649*   MAR. 30

 HE Lord summoned Moses to the top of the mountain, and Moses went up.
—Ex 19:20

REFLECTION. He went up into the mountain of contemplation, spoke to God face to face, and then came down to his brothers bearing the table of God's law, His Ladder of Perfection.

— description of *St. John Climacus,*
author of the *Ladder of Perfection*

PRAYER. *St. John, grant me the knowledge, contemplative spirit, and fortitude to climb the ladder to God.*

Bl. Joan of Toulouse +c. 14th Century*   MAR. 31

 LESSED are you who are poor for the kingdom of God is yours.
—Lk 6:20

REFLECTION. O beautiful Flower of Carmel, most fragrant vine, Splendor of Heaven, holy and remarkable, who brought forth the Son of God . . . help me in my needs.

O Star of the Sea, help and protect me!

—*St. Simon Stock*

PRAYER. *Bl. Joan, thanks to St. Simon you led a life of quiet charity. Help me to help the poor quietly, humbly.*

51

"**E** has done all things well," they said. "He even makes the deaf able to hear and the mute able to speak." —Mk 7:37

REFLECTION. My soul, have you found what you are looking for?

You were searching for God and you have found that He is the Supreme Being, and that you could never imagine anything more perfect.   —*St. Anselm*

PRAYER. *St. Hugh, though you sought solitude, God called you to ministry. May I trust that God knows the way for me.*

APR. 2   **St. Francis of Paola** +1507

THEY have pierced my hands and my feet; I can count all my bones.

—Ps 22:17

REFLECTION. Dwell on the Passion of our Lord Jesus Christ. Filled with love for us, He came down from heaven to redeem us.

He suffered every torment of body and soul for our sake.   —*St. Francis*

PRAYER. *St. Francis, your life of penance, reminds me to examine my behavior in the glorious light of Jesus' sacrifice for us.*

St. Richard +1235* APR. 3

THEY would sell their possessions and distribute to all according to what each one needed. —Acts 2:45

REFLECTION. Lord Jesus, Savior, Friend and Brother: grant that I may know You more clearly, love You more dearly, and follow You more nearly. —St. Richard

PRAYER. *St. Richard, inspire me to do without as you did so that others may have a little more.*

St. Isidore of Seville +636 APR. 4

THE Lord issues the word, and a vast army proclaims good tidings. —Ps 68:12

REFLECTION. Prayer cleanses us, reading instructs us. If we want to be God's companion, we must pray and read regularly.

When we pray, we speak to God; when we read, God speaks to us. —St. Isidore

PRAYER. *St. Isidore, author and pray-er, lead me to pray the Psalms and to read other inspired texts.*

APR. 5   St. Vincent Ferrer +1419

 THE entire community of believers was united in heart and soul.

—Acts 4:32

REFLECTION. If you desire to help the soul of your neighbor, come before God first with all your heart.

Ask God to fill you with charity, the greatest of all virtues, so that you can succeed.

—St. Vincent

PRAYER. *St. Vincent, patron of builders, may I build my life on a firm foundation of kindness.*

APR. 6   St. Irenaeus of Sirmium +304*

 DO not cast me off in my old age; do not forsake me when my strength is spent.
—Ps 71:9

REFLECTION. Lord Jesus Christ, You suffered to redeem the world because of Your compassion.

As I suffer for You and Your Church here on earth, may the heavens open and the angels receive my spirit. *—St. Irenaeus*

PRAYER. *St. Irenaeus, your final words strengthen me when I face suffering and rejection.*

St. John Baptist de la Salle +1719   APR. 7

EOPLE were bringing even infants to Jesus, so that He might touch them.

—Lk 18:15

REFLECTION. What is nobler than to form the disposition of the young?

He who knows how to shape the youthful mind is greater than painters, sculptors and all others like them.   —*St. John*

PRAYER. *St. John, teach me to cherish and nurture God's most blessed creation: children.*

St. Agabus c. First Century*   APR. 8

FTER we had been there for several days, a prophet named Agabus arrived from Judea.   —Acts 21:10

REFLECTION. "Thus says the Holy Spirit: 'This is the way the Jews in Jerusalem will bind the man who owns this belt and will hand him over to the Gentiles.'"

—*Agabus, prophesying about*
St. Paul's coming captivity

PRAYER. *St. Agabus, prophet and disciple, do not let my faith be weakened by my fears of what the future will hold.*

APR. 9 St. Gaucherius +1140*

REMBLE, O earth, at the Presence of the Lord, Who turns the rock into a pool of water and flint into a slowing spring.
—Ps 114:7-8

REFLECTION. When, consumed by love, the mind soars to God.

Blessed is the mind which, disregarding all creatures, constantly rejoiced in God's Beauty.
—*St. Maximus the Confessor*

PRAYER. *St. Gaucherius, your solitary contemplation of God leads me to seek God through prayer and meditation.*

APR. 10 St. Fulbert +1029*

O one who performs a miracle in My name will . . . speak evil of me. Whoever is not against us is for us.
—Mk 9:39-40

REFLECTION. The Church of Jesus Christ is built upon the rock of the Apostles. Despite many dangers, it therefore remains unmoved.

Waves lash at the Church but do not disturb it.
—*St. Ambrose*

PRAYER. *St. Fulbert, I give thanks for your great learning and commitment to education which helped anchor the Church.*

St. Gemma Galgani +1905*   APR. 11

 THE man said, "Teacher, I have observed all these (commandments) since I was a child." Looking at him, Jesus was moved with love. —Mk 10:20-21

REFLECTION. Help me, my Jesus, for I strive to become good whatever the cost; remove, destroy, totally root out all that You find in me contrary to Your holy will.

Empower me to walk in Your holy light. Amen.   —St. Gemma

PRAYER. *St. Gemma, I thank you for your childlike devotion to Jesus, which was wise beyond your years.*

St. Julius I +352*   APR. 12

 GIVE due honor to everyone. Love your fellow believers. Fear God. Honor the emperor. —1 Pet 2:17

REFLECTION. Do you not know that this is the custom, that we should be contacted first so that from here what is just may be defined.

     —*St. Julius, defending the primacy of the papacy*

PRAYER. *St. Julius, give me the courage to fight for what is right, the wisdom to recognize what is right, and the courtesy to conduct myself rightly.*

APR. 13 St. Martin I +656

UR soul waits in hope for the Lord; He is our help and our shield. O Lord, let Your kindness rest upon us.

—Ps 33:20, 22

REFLECTION. The Lord Himself will take care of me as He sees fit in His Divine providence, whether this means numerous sufferings or some small consolation.

Why am I afraid? The Lord is near.

—*St. Martin*

PRAYER. *St. Martin, teach me to have your extraordinary trust in God when facing pain, humiliation, and grief.*

APR. 14 St. Lydwina +1433*

LESSED are those who are persecuted in the cause of justice, for theirs is the kingdom of heaven. —Mt 5:10

REFLECTION. Many would be willing to encounter difficulties if they were not inconvenienced by them.

When distress and trouble come, do not fight them but transform them with gentleness and time. —*St. Francis de Sales*

PRAYER. *St. Lydwina, you bore afflictions with such patience. Teach me to do the same, in Jesus' name.*

St. Paternus +c. 565*   APR. 15

H E is the reflection of God's glory and the perfect expression of His very being, sustaining all things by His powerful word. —Heb 1:3

REFLECTION. Here I am, O King and Lord of all things. Unworthy but confident of Your grace and help, I offer myself entirely to You and submit all that is mine to Your will.

—*St. Ignatius of Loyola*

PRAYER. *St. Paternus, you surrendered your whole life to God's will. Teach me to submit myself to God's plan for me.*

St. Marie Bernadette Soubirous +1879*   APR. 16

A LL of these were constantly engaged in prayer, together with the women and Mary the mother of Jesus, and with His brethren. —Acts 1:14

REFLECTION. The Blessed Virgin used me as a broom to brush away the dust.

When the job is done the broom is placed behind the door and stays there.

—*St. Marie Bernadette*

PRAYER. *St. Bernadette, your witness of the Virgin Mary at Lourdes introduced the world to a miraculous healing power. Thank you!*

APR. 17   **St. Robert Molesmes** +1111*

 Y heart says of you, "Seek His face."
—Ps 27:8

REFLECTION. You helped me to know Your mercy when I lay in the dust, kissing the trace of Your sacred steps. You forgave the evil of my former life.

Then, as the day progressed, You filled Your servant's soul with rejoicing.

—*St. Bernard of Clairvaux*

PRAYER. *St. Robert, let me feel the passion you and your fellow Cistercian, St. Bernard, felt for Jesus.*

APR. 18   **Blessed Mary of the Incarnation** +1618*

 O not be afraid, daughter of Zion. Behold, your King is coming, riding on a donkey's colt. —Jn 12:15

REFLECTION. Let nothing disturb you. Let nothing frighten you. All things are passing. God alone does not change. Patience achieves everything.

Whoever has God, lacks nothing. God alone suffices. —*St. Teresa of Avila*

PRAYER. *Blessed Mary, may I follow you in being influenced by the writings of St. Teresa.*

St. Elphege +1012*   APR. 19

 JESUS answered . . ."And when I am lifted up from the earth, I will draw all to myself."   —Jn 12:32

REFLECTION. Love's precious mark, highest theme of praise, most precious light for all people.

To love Him is life; to lose Him death; to live in Him and for Him, delight. He is mine by gift; I am His by debt. —*St. Robert Southwell*

PRAYER. *St. Elphege, you died praying for your enemies. Help me to love my enemies in word and action.*

St. Agnes of Montepulciano +1317* APR. 20

 O He became as far superior to the Angels as the name He has inherited is superior to theirs.   —Heb 1:4

REFLECTION. Christ gave me a beautiful soul filled with the jewels of grace and virtue.

I belong to Him Whom the Angels serve.

—*St. Agnes*

PRAYER. *St. Agnes, the austerity of your life reminds me to make sacrifices in my own life to better follow Jesus.*

APR. 21   St. Anselm +1109

HEN it will come to pass that everyone who calls on the name of the Lord will be saved.   —Acts 2:21

REFLECTION. At this time, my Lord God, reveal to my heart where and how to seek You, where and how to find You.

If You are not here, Lord, if You are absent, where shall I look for you?   —St. Anselm

PRAYER. *St. Anselm, show me when to stand up and confront those who oppose the will of God as you did.*

APR. 22   St. Epipodius +c. 178*

HE dead . . . are no longer subject to death . . . they are children of God because they are children of the Resurrection.
                    —Lk 20:36

REFLECTION. Of what importance is it what kind of death puts an end to life, since He Who has died once will not suffer the same ordeal a second time.

The bodies of the Saints will therefore rise again free from every defect.   —St. Augustine

PRAYER. *St. Epipodius, in the face of hideous torture and martyrdom, you remained faithful. Give me such faith!*

St. George +c. 303   APR. 23

A MAN knelt down and asked Him, "Good Teacher, what must I do to inherit eternal life?" —Mk 10:17

REFLECTION. A good person is one who loves God and truly knows Him and has no peace except in doing what is pleasing to Him.

But such persons are rare.

—*St. Anthony the Great*

PRAYER. *St. George, your striving for God is legendary. Inspire me to tackle extreme challenges in doing God's work.*

St. Fidelis of Sigmaringen +1622   APR. 24

PETER answered, "Repent, and be baptized in the name of Jesus Christ so that your sins may be forgiven and you will receive the gift of the Holy Spirit." —Acts 2:38

REFLECTION. Woe to me if I should prove myself but a half-hearted soldier in the service of my thorn-crowned Captain. —*St. Fidelis*

PRAYER. *St. Fidelis, known as "the poor man's lawyer," by fighting corruption you helped the needy. May I never be half-hearted in my commitment to help those in need.*

63

APR. 25 St. Mark the Evangelist +First Century

HIS is how it is with the Kingdom of God: it is as if a man were to scatter seed on the land. —Mk 4:26

REFLECTION. Judas, one of the Twelve, came up with a crowd of men armed with swords and clubs, who had been sent by the chief priests, the scribes, and the elders.

Now the traitor had arranged a signal with them. "The one I kiss . . . arrest Him." —*St. Mark*

PRAYER. *St. Mark, I am blessed and enlightened by the inspired words you provided of Jesus and the early Church.*

APR. 26 St. Paschasius Radbertus +c. 865*

HOEVER feeds upon My flesh and drinks My blood has eternal life, and I will raise him up. —Jn 6:54

REFLECTION. Of the sacrament of the Lord's Body and Blood, every one of the faithful should be knowledgeable and aware of what in it pertains to faith and what to knowledge, because faith in the mystery is not rightly defended without knowledge, nor is knowledge nurtured without faith. —*St. Paschasius*

PRAYER. *St. Paschasius, help me to receive the Holy Eucharist with faith and knowledge.*

St. Zita +1278* APR. 27

 JESUS said, "The harvest is abundant, but the laborers are few. Therefore ask the Lord . . . to send forth laborers for His harvest."
—Mt 9:37-38

REFLECTION. A servant is not holy if she is not hard working.

Work-shy piety in people of our position is a sham. —*St. Zita*

PRAYER. *St. Zita, patron of domestic workers, help me to do my work with true piety and dedication to the Lord knowing all righteous industriousness is favorable to God.*

St. Louis Mary de Montfort +1716 APR. 28

 THE Mighty One has done great things for me and holy is His Name.
—Lk 1:49

REFLECTION. May you, O faithful Virgin, be a seal on my heart, that in you and through you I may be faithful to God.

Grant, most precious Virgin, that I may be counted among those you are pleased to love, teach, and guide. —*St. Louis*

PRAYER. *St. Louis, your devotion to Mary inspires me to ask for her intercession in my own life.*

APR. 29   St. Catherine of Siena +1380

THE Lord God formed man from the dust of the ground, and breathed into his nostrils the breath of life.   —Gen 2:7

REFLECTION. There is no way of savoring the truth and living it without self-knowledge.

It is this knowledge that makes us truly understand that we are nothing, and that our being came from God when He created us.

—*St. Catherine of Siena*

PRAYER. *St. Catherine, give me self-knowledge to understand that I have no self without God.*

APR. 30   St. Pius V +1572

AY the Lord answer you in times of trouble; may the Name of the God of Jacob protect you.   —Ps 20:2

REFLECTION. Lord Jesus crucified, Son of the most blessed Virgin Mary, open Your ears and listen to me as You listened to God the Father.

Lord Jesus crucified . . . open Your blessed mouth and speak to me as You spoke to St. John.   —*St. Pius*

PRAYER. *St. Pius, give me the voice to call upon Jesus for help during times of trouble and conflict.*

St. Jeremiah +586 B.C.* MAY 1

YOU surely must have heard of the mystery of God's grace that was entrusted to me on your behalf, and how the mystery was made known to me by a revelation.

—Eph 3:2-3

REFLECTION. O Lord, be with me, and defend me from those who persecute me. Your words bring joy and gladness to my heart.

O Lord, my power, my strength, and my shelter in the day of tribulation: to You the Gentiles shall come from all the ends of the earth.

—*St. Jeremiah*

PRAYER. *St. Jeremiah, help me to take joy in the word of God just as you did.*

St. Athanasius +373 MAY 2

HOW can you say, ". . . let me remove the splinter that is in your eye," while all the time you do not notice the wooden plank that is in your own eye? —Lk 6:42

REFLECTION. We often do things thoughtlessly. The Lord, however, sees everything. Therefore, leaving judgment to Him, we must have compassion for one another.

Bearing one another's burdens, we must also examine ourselves closely to improve the areas in which we are lacking. —*St. Athanasius*

PRAYER. *St. Athanasius, help me to recognize my failings and seek daily to mend my ways.*

67

St. James +62 **MAY 3**

F your brother wrongs you, go and take up the matter with him when the two of you are alone. If he listens to you, you have won your brother over. —Mt 18:15

REFLECTION. Do not forget that everyone should be quick to listen, but slow to speak and slow to anger.

For human anger does not bring about the righteousness of God. So rid yourselves of everything sordid and of every evil excess.

—*St. James*

PRAYER. *Saint James, help me to put aside my anger and seek to be gentle in all that I do.*

St. Florian +c. 304 **MAY 4**

N the daytime, He led them with a cloud, and all night long, with a fiery light.

—Ps 78:14

REFLECTION. We were so utterly unbearably crushed that we despaired of life itself. Indeed, we felt that we had received the sentence of death so that we would rely not on ourselves but on God, Who raises the dead. —*St. Paul*

PRAYER. *St. Florian, let me be on fire with love for Christ, and let me light up faith and hope in all those I meet.*

St. Gothard (Godehard) +1038*　　　**MAY 5**

OWEVER, it is God who enables both us and you to stand firm in Christ.
　　　　　　　　　　　　　　—2 Cor 1:21-22

REFLECTION.　　The duty of the Word is to oversee our instruction and discipline. Therefore, work hard and don't grow weary.

How can we not acknowledge the Divine Instructor with the utmost gratitude?
　　　　　　　　　　—St. Clement of Alexandria

PRAYER.　*St. Gothard, help me to live my faith with fortitude and follow the guidance sent me from the Lord.*

St. Edbert +698*　　　　　　**MAY 6**

OR whoever wishes to save his life will lose it, but whoever loses his life for My sake . . . will save it.　　　　**—Mk 8:35**

REFLECTION.　　Do not listen to those who say we need only our own free will and not prayer to keep us from sin.

It isn't a question of prayers alone; we need to include our deliberate efforts.

　　　　　　　　　　　　　—Saint Augustine

PRAYER.　*St. Edbert, as bishop, you lead your people to greater piety. Help me to use the proper combination of prayer, fasting, and action to follow Jesus.*

Bl. Giselle +1060*   MAY 7

 ESUS said, "Behold My mother and My brethren. Whoever does the will of God is my brother and sister and mother."

—Mk 3:34-35

REFLECTION. Think of yourself always as the servant of all.

Christ has no body now on earth but yours; yours are the eyes through which Christ's compassion looks out at the world.—*St. Teresa of Avila*

PRAYER. *Blessed Giselle, help me, whatever state I find myself in, to serve those in need.*

St. Desideratus +550*   MAY 8

 ESUS replied, "I am the Way, and the Truth, and the Life. No one comes to the Father except through Me."   —Jn 14:6

REFLECTION. He Who is the Way doesn't deceive us or lead us into spacious wastelands. He who is the Truth doesn't taunt us with lies. He who is the Life doesn't betray us with deathly delusions.

Christ chose these names for Himself to show us His plan for our salvation.

—*St. Hilary of Poitiers*

PRAYER. *St. Desideratus, help me to draw all those I know closer to Jesus by the way I live.*

St. Isaiah +Eighth Century B.C.*

 AM the good shepherd. I know My own, and My own know Me, just as the Father knows Me and I know the Father. —Jn 10:14-15

REFLECTION. Behold the Lord God comes with strength, to rule. . . . He shall feed His flock like a shepherd; gathering together the lambs in His arms, carrying them close to His heart.

—*St. Isaiah*

PRAYER. *St. Isaiah, help me, in my own humble speech, to lead people to Jesus Christ, the Messiah.*

St. John of Avila +1569*

 AIT quietly for the Lord, and be patient until He comes. Do not fret over the man who prospers because of his evil schemes. —Ps 37:7

REFLECTION. Christ tells us that if we want to join Him we should follow His way.

It is not right that the Son of God should take the path of shame while we walk the way of worldly honor. —*St. John of Avila*

PRAYER. *St. John, help me to use what is in my wallet and in my heart for others.*

St. Francis di Girolamo +1716*   **MAY 11**

 LESSED is the man who perseveres when he is tempted, for when he has been proven he will receive the crown of life.   **—Jas 1:12**

REFLECTION.   If we wish to be saved, let us lose our lives to the world as those who have been crucified with Christ.

Let us glory in the cross of our Lord, Jesus Christ.   *—St. Francis*

PRAYER.   *St. Francis, help me to become more selfless so that I may live as one who is given up to Christ.*

Sts. Nereus and Achilleus +Third Century **MAY 12**

 LESSED are the peacemakers, for they shall be called children of God.
   —Mt 5:9

REFLECTION.   O miracle of faith! Suddenly they cease their fury and desert their wicked leader. They throw away their shields, their armor and their blood-stained spears.

Confessing their faith in Christ, they rejoice to bear testimony to its triumph.
   —Pope Damasus: Epitaph for Nereus and Achilleus

PRAYER.   *Saints Nereus and Achilleus, help me to be faithful, even if it means changing my life to stay consistent with my beliefs.*

Bl. Juliana of Norwich +c. 1423*   **MAY 13**

 JESUS said, "Amen, I say to you, unless you change and become like little children, you will never enter the kingdom of heaven."

—Mt 18:3

REFLECTION. I saw that He is to us everything that is good and comfortable for us.

He is our clothing that for love wraps us, clasps us, and bedclothes us for tender love, that He may never leave us.   *—Blessed Juliana*

PRAYER. *Blessed Juliana, you experienced revelations of God's extraordinary love. Help me to remember how completely God loves me.*

St. Matthias +First Century   **MAY 14**

 THEY prayed, . . . "Show us which one of these two You have chosen to take the place . . . that Judas abandoned" . . . They cast lots and the lot fell to Matthias who was then added to the eleven.

—Acts 1:24-26

REFLECTION. As the leader the of Apostles, Peter always took the initiative in speaking (but) he left the decision to all of them.

But it was Peter who presented the idea, pointing out that it was not his own but had been suggested to him by a scriptural prophecy.

—St. John Chrysostom

PRAYER. *St. Matthias, help me to know when God is choosing me and to accept His invitation.*

73

MAY 15   St. Isidore +c. 1130

O all of you who are God's beloved in Rome: grace to you and peace from God our Father and the Lord Jesus Christ.

—Rom 1:7

REFLECTION. Any teaching, that is not supported by grace may enter our ears, but it never reaches the heart.

When God's grace does touch our innermost minds, then His word can move deep into our heart.   —St. Isidore

PRAYER. *St. Isidore, your care for the poor reflected God's grace. Help me to welcome all opportunities to accept grace.*

MAY 16   St. Brendan +c. 577*

ND when He got into the boat, His disciples followed Him. A windstorm arose on the sea.   —Mt 8:23-24

REFLECTION. And now, my Lord, reveal to my heart where and how to seek you, where and how to find you.

If, Lord, You are not here, where shall I look for You?   —St. Anselm

PRAYER. *St. Brendan, Patron of Sailors, you made many journeys to evangelize. Help me to go wherever I'm needed to spread the word of God.*

74

St. Paschal Baylon +1592*   **MAY 17**

 HEN He took bread and after giving thanks, broke it and gave it to them, saying, "This is My body which will be given for you. Do this in memory of Me." —Lk 22:19

REFLECTION. I desire to love You my Lord, my Light, my Strength, my Deliverer, my God, and my All.

My spirit and my body yearn for Your majesty. —*St. Paschal Baylon*

PRAYER. *St. Paschal, help me to love the Holy Eucharist and yearn for the Holy Presence just as you did.*

———————

St. John I +526   **MAY 18**

 ETER said to Him, ". . . I will lay down my life for you." Jesus answered, "Will you really lay down your life for Me?" —Jn 13:37-38

REFLECTION. Martyrdom makes disciples like their Master, who willingly accepted death for the salvation of the world, and through it they are made like Him by the shedding of blood.

Therefore, the Church considers it the highest gift and supreme test of love.

—*Dogmatic Constitution of the Church, 42*

PRAYER. *St. John, Pope and martyr, help me to make the sacrifices I must make to serve Christ.*

MAY 19 St. Yves +1303*

OR the one whom God has sent speaks the words of God.

—Jn 3:34

REFLECTION. These are the words of Christ, "Call no man master for you are all brothers."

Going to the people is the purest and best act in Christian tradition and revolutionary tradition and is the beginning of world brotherhood. —*Dorothy Day*

PRAYER. *St. Yves, as a lawyer and a priest, you were the "poor man's advocate." May I use my resources to help the poor.*

MAY 20 St. Bernardine of Sienna +1444

HEN Agrippa said to Paul, "Do you think that in such a brief time you can persuade me to become a Christian?"

—Acts 26:28

REFLECTION. When a fire is lit to clear a field, it burns off all the dry and useless weeds.

So when Paul's voice was raised to preach the Gospel, like a great clap of thunder in the sky, his preaching was a blazing fire carrying all before it. —*St. Bernardine*

PRAYER. *St. Bernardine, you rejected all honors with humility. Help me to humbly use my gifts to advance the Gospel.*

Saint Eugene de Mazenod +1861* **MAY 21**

HE Spirit of Truth who comes from the Father will testitfy on my behalf.

—Jn 15:26

REFLECTION. We are not trained for war but for peace. In war there is need for much equipment. But peace and love . . . do not need weapons or abundant supplies.

Their sustenance is the word.

—*St. Clement of Alexandria*

PRAYER. *St. Eugene, you founded missionary orders that brought Christianity to the world. May I bring the word of God to those I encounter.*

St. Rita of Cascia +c. 1457 **MAY 22**

UT when I stumbled, they rejoiced and came together; they came together and struck me unawares. They slandered me.

—Ps 35:15

REFLECTION. The more we indulge ourselves in comfort and pamper our bodies, the more they will rebel against the spirit.

O loving Jesus, increase my patience as my sufferings increase. —*St. Rita*

PRAYER. *St. Rita, remind me that my suffering is nothing compared to what Christ suffered for me.*

MAY 23 St. John Baptist Dei Rossi +1764*

 OR I am fully aware of my offense, and my sin is ever before me. Against You alone have I sinned. —Ps 51:5-6

REFLECTION. O Jesus, my Redeemer . . . since You continued to pursue me, even after I turned away from You, I do not fear that You will reject me now that I seek to love You with all my heart. I am sorry for having offended You. —St. Alphonsus de'Liguori

PRAYER. *St. John, you drew people to Jesus through the sacrament of confession. Help me to seek the healing of this sacrament.*

MAY 24 St. Donatian and St. Rogatian +c. 304*

 OR if we have been united with Him in a death like His, we shall also be united with Him in His resurrection. —Rom 6:5

REFLECTION. Oh, if all were to know how beautiful Jesus is, how amiable He is!

They would all die of love.

—St. Gemma Galgani

PRAYER. *Sts. Donatian and Rogatian, you remained true to your beliefs, even when it cost you everything. Help me to remain faithful to Jesus at all costs.*

St. Bede the Venerable +735   **MAY 25**

 CONTINUALLY give thanks to my God for you because of the grace of God that has been given you in Christ Jesus.   —1 Cor 1:4

REFLECTION.   We journey towards the light of our celestial home, illumined and guided by Christ's grace.

This light of grace was prefigured by the pillar of cloud and fire which protected the children of Israel . . . and led them to the land they had been promised.   —St. Bede

PRAYER.   *St. Bede, help me faithfully explore my place in the Word and the world.*

St. Philip Neri +1595   **MAY 26**

 PLACE my trust in You my God, my life is in Your hands.

—Ps 31:15, 16

REFLECTION.   Lord, take care of me, lest I betray You if You do not help me.

Do with me, Lord, as You will and know to be best.   —*St. Philip Neri*

PRAYER.   *St. Philip Neri, you were deeply aware of the need for penance and God's mercy. May I turn always to God in my weakness, seeking His strength.*

MAY 27 St. Augustine of Canterbury +605

 O faith by itself, if it has no works, is dead. For just as the body without the spirit is dead, so faith without works is also dead.
—Jas 2:17, 26

REFLECTION. They bow down in prayer to free their minds of earthly things. Whose achievement is this?

It is the achievement of Him who said, "My Father is at work until now, and I am at work as well." —*St. Augustine of Canterbury*

PRAYER. *St. Augustine, you zealously established Christianity in England. Help me to work for Christianity wherever I am sent.*

MAY 28   St. Germanus +576*

 NLY goodness and kindness will follow me all the days of my life, and I will dwell in the house of the Lord forever.
—Ps 23:6

REFLECTION. Charity is the bond of a community, the foundation of peace. It is greater than both faith and hope; it surpasses both good works and suffering for the faith; and will abide with us forever in the kingdom of heaven. —*St. Cyprian*

PRAYER. *St. Germanus, your steadfast charity converted kings and commoners. Teach me charity even when challenged by the world and its leaders.*

St. Maximinus of Trier +c. 346*   MAY 29

 N the beginning was the Word, and the Word was with God, and the Word was God.
—Jn 1:1

REFLECTION. We do not worship a creature. Far be that from us!

We worship the Lord of creation, Incarnate, the Word of God.   —*St. Athanasius*

PRAYER. *St. Maximinus, you sheltered saints like Athanasius and battled unbelievers. May I embody true faith and hospitality.*

St. Joan of Arc +1431*   MAY 30

 LORD, my God, I take refuge in You; keep me safe from all my pursuers and deliver me, lest like a lion they tear me to pieces.   —Ps 7:2-3

REFLECTION. We must run from sin to righteousness. In the same way, those who practice righteousness must beware lest they open themselves up to sin.

Our struggle in this world is short.

—*Sulpitius Severus*

PRAYER. *St. Joan of Arc, your short life was focused on righteousness. Help me to follow God's plan for my life.*

MAY 31 Feast of the Visitation of the Blessed Virgin Mary

 LIZABETH was filled with the Holy Spirit and cried out in a loud voice: "Blessed are you among women, and blessed is the fruit of your womb." —Lk 1:41-42

REFLECTION. "My soul proclaims the greatness of the Lord, and my spirit rejoices in God my Savior.

"For the Almighty has done great things for me, and Holy is His name." —*Mary, Mother of Jesus*

PRAYER. *Mary, mother of all God's children, just as you hastened to help your cousin, Elizabeth, help me hurry to aid all my brothers and sisters in need.*

JUNE 1 St. Justin +165

 OR this I was born, and for this I came into the world, to testify to the truth. —Jn 18:37a

REFLECTION. It is our duty to teach our doctrine, or incur the guilt and the punishment of those who sin through ignorance.

No honest person forsakes truth for falsehood. —*St. Justin*

PRAYER. *St. Justin, help me to seek true understanding of the faith just as you did, and help me to commit my life to Christ.*

St. Stephen of Sweden +c. 1075*   JUNE 2

HE wicked man keeps close watch on the righteous and seeks an opportunity to kill him. —Ps 37:32

REFLECTION.
The martyrs' triumph let us sing,
Their blood poured forth for Christ the King,
And while due hymns of praise we pray,
Our thankful hearts cast grief away.

—*St. Ambrose*

PRAYER. *St. Stephen, you died fighting idolatry. Let me avoid making money and possessions into idols that keep me from God.*

Sts. Charles Lwanga   JUNE 3
and Companions +1886, 1887

E ourselves, who have the firstfruits of the Spirit, groan inwardly as we wait for our adoption as children, the redemption of our bodies. —Rom 8:23

REFLECTION. Saint Charles and his companions inaugurate a new age.

Africa is the new Christian territory. A clear witness of this fact is the complete simplicity and unshakable faith of these young African Christians. —*Pope Paul VI*

PRAYER. *St. Charles, following your example may I encourage new Christians of every race and ethnicity.*

83

JUNE 4   St. Francis Caracciolo +1608*

 MAN with leprosy approached, knelt before Him, and said, "Lord, if You choose to do so, You can make me clean."

—Mt 8:2

REFLECTION. Since this house is open to all, it receives the sick of every kind: the crippled, the disabled, lepers, mutes, the insane, . . . and those bearing the affliction of old age.

No payment is required; Christ provides what is needed. —*St. John of God*

PRAYER. *St. Francis Caracciolo, you served lepers. Help me never to turn my face or hand from those whom society rejects.*

JUNE 5   St. Boniface +754

 UT You, O Lord, are a shield to protect me; You are my glory and the One Who raises my head high. —Ps 3:4

REFLECTION. Let us be steadfast in what is right and prepare our souls for judgment. Let us await God's powerful aid and say to Him, "O Lord, You have been our refuge in all generations."

Let us trust Him Who places this call upon us. —*St. Boniface*

PRAYER. *St. Boniface, like you, may I have the courage to speak the Gospel to those who do not yet believe.*

St. Norbert +1134 JUNE 6

"**L**ORD," Peter said to Him, "You know everything. You know that I love You." Jesus said to him, "Feed my sheep." —Jn 21:17

REFLECTION. O Priest! You are not your own because you are God's . . . because you are Christ's servant.

You are not your own because you are the spouse of the Church. You are not your own because you are the mediator between God and man. —*St. Norbert*

PRAYER. *St. Norbert, you relied on the power of God. Remind me that without God I can do nothing; I am nothing.*

Bl. Anne of St. Bartholomew +1626* JUNE 7

BLESSED are the poor in spirit, for theirs is the kingdom of heaven.

—Mt 5:3

REFLECTION. Blessed God, I know that whoever undertakes anything for the sake of material things, or to earn the praise of others, is deceived. Today, one thing pleases us; tomorrow, it is another. —*St. Teresa of Avila*

PRAYER. *Bl. Anne, you rejected the world to serve St. Teresa and the Carmelites. Help me to turn away from evil and to choose what is good.*

JUNE 8 St. Medard +561*

 ESUS instructed them to take nothing for their journey except a walking staff—no bread, no sack, no money. —Mk 6:8

REFLECTION. By trusting God, we won't fall into sin, lust after anything, resent anyone, or store up earthly treasure.

By expecting death, we will surrender riches and forgive everyone for everything.

—St. Athanasius

PRAYER. *St. Medard, for over a century, you served Christ. Help me respect the wisdom of my elders in faith.*

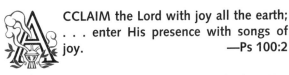

JUNE 9 St. Ephrem +378

CCLAIM the Lord with joy all the earth; . . . enter His presence with songs of joy. —Ps 100:2

REFLECTION. In the sacrament of the Eucharist we embrace You and receive You into our bodies. Help us to be worthy to experience the resurrection for which we hope.

We have had Your treasure hidden within us through the grace of baptism. —St. Ephrem

PRAYER. *St. Ephrem, your beautiful hymns led you to be called "The Harp of the Holy Spirit." Help me to ever sing the praises of God.*

St. Landericus +656*　　　　JUNE 10

SELL everything you own and distribute the money to the poor, and you will have treasure in heaven. Then come, follow Me.

—Lk 18:22

REFLECTION.　If we share with the poor out of the love of God whatever He has given us, we shall receive according to His promise a hundredfold in eternal happiness.

What a great profit, what a blessed reward!

—*St. John of God*

PRAYER.　*St. Landericus, you sold your possessions to establish a hospital for the poor. Lead me to serve the sick and the poor.*

St. Barnabas +First Century　　　　JUNE 11

THUS Joseph, also named Barnabas meaning "son of encouragement" . . . sold a field and then brought the money and put it at the feet of the Apostles.

—Acts 4:36-37

REFLECTION.　We are of the same nature as you, human beings.

We announce the good news that you should turn from these idols to the living God.

—*Sts. Barnabas and Paul*

PRAYER.　*St. Barnabas, may I stand for Christ before those who worship the idols of our world, as you did.*

JUNE 12　　　St. Leo III +816*

HEN you have lifted up the Son of Man, then you will know that I AM, that I do nothing on My own authority. —Jn 8:28

REFLECTION. For he [the Pope] is believed to be the representative of Christ . . . and for that reason is called by a name of the Lord, according to the words of the Apostle, "You have received the spirit of adoption of sons whereby we cry, Abba, Father." —St. Benedict

PRAYER. *St. Leo, you were devoted to the divinity of Christ as Son of the Father. Help me embrace my adoption as a child of God.*

JUNE 13　　　St. Anthony of Padua +1231

LL of them were filled with the Holy Spirit and began to speak in different languages, as the Spirit enabled them to do so. —Acts 2:4

REFLECTION. Those who are filled with the Holy Spirit speak in different languages.

These different languages are different ways of giving witness to Christ, such as humility, poverty, patience, and obedience.

—St. Anthony

PRAYER. *St. Anthony, your preaching inspired many believers. Give me the words to draw people to Christ.*

St. Methodius +847*   **JUNE 14**

 HY, O Lord, do You stand far off? Why do You remain hidden in times of trouble? —Ps 10:1

REFLECTION. I long for You, God of our holy Fathers and Lord of Mercy. I seek You, the Author of all life.

With great longing I expect You, Who, with Your word, embraces all things. I wait for You, the Lord of Life and Death.   —*St. Methodius*

PRAYER. *St. Methodius, you became a Patriarch after years of persecution. Help me to love those who insult me for my love of Christ.*

St. Germaine Cousin +1601*   **JUNE 15**

 OW forceful are honest words! But your reproof, what does it reprove? You would even cast lots over the orphan, and bargain over your friend. —Job 6:25, 27

REFLECTION. When you experience humiliation, you should take it as a sure sign that some grace will be yours.

Who is free from imperfections? He lacks everything who thinks he lacks nothing.

—*St. Bernard*

PRAYER. *St. Germaine, you were abused by those who should have loved you. Help me to turn to God when I feel betrayed.*

89

JUNE 16　　　　**St. Lutgardis** +1246*

 ECAUSE of the tender mercy of our God by which the dawn from on high will break upon us to shine on those who sit in . . . the shadow of death.　　　　**—Lk 1:78-79**

REFLECTION.　Before the brilliant sun becomes darkened in the sky; let Your light appear, and take away the gloom that diminishes my intellect.

Have mercy on me, O Lord, for You are abundant in mercy!　　　*—St. Ephrem the Syrian*

PRAYER.　*St. Lutgardis, while blind, you healed; while sightless, you saw visions. Let me see my limits through God's kind eyes.*

JUNE 17　　**St. Theresa of Portugal** +1250*

 HOEVER wishes to be great among you must be your servant, and whoever wishes to be first among you must be your servant.　**—Mt 20:26-27**

REFLECTION.　I imagine that my soul and body are like the two hands of a compass, and that my soul, like the stationary hand, is fixed in Jesus, Who is my center, and that my body, like the moving hand, is evidence of my assignments and obligations.

—St. Anthony Mary Claret

PRAYER.　*St. Theresa, devoted mother, queen, and daughter of God, help me to set my priorities in accord with the Lord.*

St. Gregory Barbarigo +1697*   JUNE 18

 IS IT lawful to do good or evil on the Sabbath? To save life or to kill?

—Mk 3:4

REFLECTION. You must always have prudence and love. Prudence has the eyes; love has the legs.

Love impels us to run to God, but the impulse to rush toward Him is blind and at times we would stumble, if we were not guided by prudence.   —Padre Pio

PRAYER. *St. Gregory, you guided your diocese with wisdom and prudence. Help me to temper my enthusiasm with God's guidance.*

St. Romuald +c. 1027   JUNE 19

 TO the pure all things are pure, but to those who are corrupt and without faith nothing is pure.   —Tit 1:15

REFLECTION. An evil thought, for those who dismiss it, is a sign of their love of God and not of sin; for the thought itself is not sin, but friendly converse of the mind with it.

—St. Mark the Ascetic

PRAYER. *St. Romuald, strengthened by solitude, you built monasteries and fought temptation. Strengthen me in my baptismal vows to reject sin and temptation.*

JUNE 20 St. Methodius of Alypius +c. 312*

HOEVER loves Me will keep My word, and My Father will love him, and We will come to him and make Our abode with him.   —Jn 14:23

REFLECTION.   Blessed and Eternal Father, bringing all creation together by Your strength, making the heavens Your abode: May we also pass through the gates of life, welcomed by You and Your Son.   —*St. Methodius*

PRAYER. *St. Methodius, inspired by your writing, help me to keep a prayer diary in which I record my love of God.*

JUNE 21   St. Aloysius Gonzaga +1591

OU are now in anguish, but I will see you again, and your hearts will rejoice, and no one shall deprive you of your joy.   —Jn 16:22

REFLECTION.   Our parting will not be for long; we shall see each other again in heaven and be united with our Savior.

There we shall praise Him with heart and soul, sing of His mercies and enjoy happiness with Him forever.   —*St. Aloysius*

PRAYER. *St. Aloysius, you maintained purity and innocence amid corruption. May I remain pure in a corrupt world.*

St. Thomas More +1535   JUNE 22

LL you peoples, clap your hands, shout to God with cries of gladness. For the Lord, . . . is awesome; He is the great King over all the earth. —Ps 47:2-3

REFLECTION. God gave us the grace to deny our self and to fully depend upon the hope and strength of God.

The meeker a person is, the more is God's strength evident in safeguarding him.

—*St. Thomas More*

PRAYER. *St. Thomas, as a powerful advocate for God, help me never to let my ambitions come between me and the Father.*

St. Ethelreda +679*   JUNE 23

O not let your hearts be troubled. You place your trust in God. Trust also in Me. —Jn 14:1

REFLECTION. Peace does not reside in outward things, but within one's soul; we may maintain it in the midst of the bitterest pain, if our will remains firm and submissive.

Peace in this life springs from obedience, not in the absence of suffering.

— *Francois Fenelon*

PRAYER. *St. Ethelreda, let me recognize in my sufferings the opportunity to grow nearer to the Lord as you did.*

JUNE 24 Nativity of St. John the Baptist

+First Century

ND you, O child, shall be called prophet of the Most High; for you shall go before the Lord to prepare straight paths for Him. —Lk 1:76

REFLECTION. Bear fruits worthy of repentance . . . every tree therefore that does not bear good fruit is cut down and thrown into the fire.

Whoever has two coats must share with anyone who has none; and whoever has food should do likewise. —*St. John the Baptist*

PRAYER. *St. John, you prepared the way for Jesus by telling us how to live. Help me to bear good fruit by my actions.*

JUNE 25 St. Prosper +c. 465*

OR all have sinned and are thereby deprived of the glory of God, and all are justified by the gift of His grace, that is given freely through the redemption in Christ Jesus. —Rom 3:23-24

REFLECTION. Scripture clearly demonstrates, I think, that the faith which justifies a sinner is God's gift to us and is not a reward for previous merits. —*St. Prosper*

PRAYER. *St. Prosper, you remind us that faith is a gift from God. Help me to value and nurture this gift, by the grace of God.*

St. Josemaria Escriva +1975*   JUNE 26

 UT I say this to you: . . . Whoever addresses his brother in an insulting way will answer for it.

—Mt 5:22

REFLECTION. Never respond while you are still angry about a situation—wait until the next day, or even longer.

And then calmly, and with a pure intention, make your response. You will gain more by a friendly word than by a lengthy argument.

—St. Josemaria

PRAYER. *St. Josemaria, you counseled against anger. Help me to stifle any impulses of anger or unkindness.*

St. Cyril of Alexandria +444   JUNE 27

 E speak of these things in words taught to us . . . by the Spirit, expressing spiritual things in spiritual words.

—1 Cor 2:13

REFLECTION. Divinely inspired Scriptures affirm that the Word of God was made flesh, that is to say, Jesus Christ was united to a human body endowed with a rational soul.

We believe, therefore, that there is in Emmanuel two entities, divinity and humanity.

—St. Cyril

PRAYER. *St. Cyril, your defense of Mary as the mother of God brought you persecution. Help me to defend the truths of my faith in an unbelieving world.*

JUNE 28 **St. Irenaeus** +202

 HOEVER has seen Me, has seen the Father. . . . I am in the Father and the Father is in Me. —Jn 14:9-10

REFLECTION. God, Who brings about all things, is invisible and inexplicable, both in His power and His greatness.

From the beginning, the Son reveals the Father. —*St. Irenaeus*

PRAYER. *St. Irenaeus, you remind us that Jesus shows us the Father. Help me recognize the Word of God in the Son of God.*

JUNE 29 **St. Peter** +First Century

 O humble yourselves under the mighty hand of God, so that at the proper time He may exalt you. Cast your worries upon Him because He cares for you. —1 Pet 5:6

REFLECTION. But to attain this, you will have to surpass yourselves, adding goodness to the faith you have, understanding to the goodness, self-control to your understanding, patience to your self-control, true devotion to your patience, kindness . . . and to this kindness, love. —*St. Peter*

PRAYER. *St. Peter, you understood our frailties because you had been frail. Help me to assist those who are frailer in their faith than I.*

The First Holy Martyrs of the Church +64 JUNE 30

IF the world hates you, be aware that it hated Me before it hated you. . . . I have chosen you . . . therefore the world hates you.

—Jn 15:18-19

REFLECTION. It was through envy and jealousy that the greatest and most dedicated Christians were persecuted and put to death.

But they courageously completed the test of faith and despite their bodily weakness won a noble prize. *—Pope Clement I*

PRAYER. *I pray that I may never have to give my life for my faith, but I ask for the courage to give whatever I must give for Christ.*

Bl. Junipero Serra +1784 JULY 1

YOU will be my witnesses not only in Jerusalem, but throughout Judea and Samaria, and indeed to the farthest ends of the earth. *—Acts 1:8*

REFLECTION. I wish I could put into words the great joy that fills my heart.

Relying on these words would always encourage me to go forward and never turn back. *—Bl. Junipero Serra*

PRAYER. *Bl. Junipero, you were a true missionary. Help me to spread the Word of God in my home, work, and travels.*

JULY 2   St. Bernardino Realino +1616*

RETHREN, I could not talk to you as spiritual people, but as worldly, as infants in Christ.   —1 Cor 3:1

REFLECTION.   Listen to me, you that pursue righteousness, you that seek the Lord.

Look to the rock from which you were hewn, and to the quarry from which you were dug.   —*St. Isaiah*

PRAYER.   *St. Bernardino, just as you ministered to young people, help me to be an example and encouragement to youthful faith.*

JULY 3   St. Thomas +First Century

HEN Jesus said to [Thomas], "You . . . believe because you have seen Me. Blessed are those who have not seen and yet . . . believe."   —Jn 20:29

REFLECTION.   God cannot be seen by man.

Thomas saw a human whom he acknowledged to be God, and said, "My Lord and my God."   —*St. Gregory the Great*

PRAYER.   *St. Thomas, may I move from doubt, to belief, to service, just as you did.*

St. Ulric +973*   JULY 4

LORD, our Lord, how glorious is Your name in all the earth! You have exalted Your majesty above the heavens. What is man, that You are mindful of him?
—Ps 8:2, 5

REFLECTION. Take away the fuel, and you take away the fire. —St. Ulric

PRAYER. *St. Ulric, as bishop, you were ceaseless in your efforts to preserve and strengthen your diocese. Help me to recognize the efficacy of prayer and the necessity of action.*

St. Anthony Zaccaria +1539   JULY 5

UT I say to you: Love your enemies and pray for those who persecute you.
—Mt 5:45

REFLECTION. In His mercy God has chosen us, unworthy as we are, out of the world to serve Him. We go forth in goodness to bear the greatest possible purity of love in patience. —St. Anthony

PRAYER. *St. Anthony, physician and priest, teach me to heal bodies and souls in my volunteer work.*

JULY 6   St. Maria Goretti +1902

 ET the little children come to Me; do not hinder them. For it is to such as these that the kingdom of God belongs. Whoever does not receive the kingdom of God like a little child will never enter it. —Mk 10:14-15

REFLECTION. Even if she had not been a martyr, she would still have been a saint, so holy was the everyday life of Maria Goretti.

—*Cardinal Salotti*

PRAYER. *St. Maria, you were killed as a child because you would not surrender to another's sin. Give me the purity and strength to resist being tempted to sin by others.*

JULY 7   St. Ethelburga +c. 600*

 IMPLORE you . . . by the mercies of God, to offer your bodies as a living sacrifice, holy, acceptable to God,—a spiritual act of worship. —Rom 12:1

REFLECTION. No one can make poor those He makes rich, for those who have been supplied with heavenly food can't be poor.

For those who are being perfected, elaborate and costly houses will seem dull in comparison to the dwelling in which God has lived.

—*St. Cyprian*

PRAYER. *St. Ethelburga, let me live in God's dwelling-place by carrying it within me.*

St. Prisca and St. Aquila +First Century*

YOUR obedience has become known to all and has caused me to rejoice greatly over you. —Rom 16:19

REFLECTION. Give my greetings to Prisca and Aquila, my co-workers in Christ Jesus, who have risked their lives for me.

Greet also the Church that assembles in their house. —*St. Paul*

PRAYER. *Sts. Prisca and Aquila, remind me to open my heart, mind, and home to Jesus and His teachers.*

Sts. Augustine Zhao Rong and JULY 9
Martyred Companions +1648-1930

DESPITE what other people do, I have been guided by the word of Your lips and refrained from their acts of violence. —Ps 17:4

REFLECTION. The precepts of the Lord give joy to the heart. These words reflect the experience of Augustine Zhao Rong and his 119 companions.

Their testimonies allow us to glimpse a state of mind marked by deep serenity and joy. —*Pope John Paul II*

PRAYER. *From the Martyrs of China, I ask courage to stand for Christ against any government.*

101

WOULD know nothing except Jesus Christ—
and Him crucified. I came to you in weakness, in fear, and in great trepidation.

—1 Cor 2:2-3

REFLECTION.   When we endure evils courageously, our long-suffering comes from Christ.

So if personal pleasures do not captivate us, and if we are not frightened by brutality, then we have overcome the world.   —St. Augustine

PRAYER. *St. Canute, as king, you died fighting for the Church. Help me appreciate all martyrs who have protected the Church.*

JULY 11   **St. Benedict** +547

 HEN a man came forward and asked Him, "Teacher, what good things must I do to achieve eternal life?"   —Mt 19:16

REFLECTION.   Through faith and good works, let us follow the path of Christ by the guidance of the Holy Gospel.

If we wish to have a place in His kingdom, our progress will be improved by our good deeds.   —St. Benedict

PRAYER. *St. Benedict, let me be disciplined in my faith, strengthened in my prayers, and charitable in my actions.*

St. John Gualbert +1073*   **JULY 12**

FOR even the Son of Man did not come to be served but to serve and to give His life as a ransom for many.   —Mk 10:45

REFLECTION. To those who would inflict heavy punishment on captives I respond, "Allow the murderer to live so that he can be saved."

That is our purpose here.   —*Bl. Junipero Serra*

PRAYER. *St. John, you forgave your brother's murderer. May my forgiveness of others lead to their salvation and mine.*

St. Henry II +1024   **JULY 13**

GIVE to Caesar what is due to Caesar, and to God what is due to God.   —Mt 22:21

REFLECTION. We encourage our children to take an active part in public life and to contribute toward the attainment of the common good of the entire human family.

Every believer must be a spark of light, a center of love, a vivifying leaven among his fellow men.   —*Pope John XXIII*

PRAYER. *St. Henry, remind me to be a Christian in my daily life for the good of the world.*

JULY 14   Bl. Kateri Tekakwitha +1680

PURSUE righteousness, faith, love, and peace together with those who call on the Lord with a pure heart. —2 Tim 2:22

REFLECTION. I am not my own; I have given myself to Jesus. He must be my only love. The state of helpless poverty that may befall me if I do not marry does not frighten me.

He will have mercy on me and help me, I am sure. —*Bl. Kateri*

PRAYER. *Bl. Kateri, your devotion to Jesus inspires me. Help my trust in the Lord to increase.*

JULY 15   St. Bonaventure +1274

WHENEVER you pray, do not be like the hypocrites who love to stand and pray . . . so that others may observe them doing so. —Mt 6:5

REFLECTION. Prayer consists in turning the mind to God.

When you pray gather up your whole self, enter with your Beloved into the chamber of your heart, and there remain with Him, forgetting all your concerns. —*St. Bonaventure*

PRAYER. *St. Bonaventure, when I pray, help me to focus my entire being on the Lord.*

Our Lady of Mount Carmel   JULY 16

THE mother of Jesus said to Him, "They have no wine." . . . (She) said to the servants, "Do whatever He tells you."

—Jn 2:3, 5

REFLECTION.   Take this scapular. Whosoever dies wearing it shall not suffer eternal fire.

It shall be a sign of salvation, a protection in danger, and a pledge of peace.

—*Our Lady of Carmel*

PRAYER.   *Lady of Mount Carmel, please intercede with your Son for me and draw me closer to Him in all that I do and all that I am.*

St. Marcellina +c. 398*   JULY 17

TO everyone who has, more will be given, but from the one who has not, even what he does have will be taken away."

—Lk 19:26

REFLECTION.   Don't hide your talent, but like a good business person, always work with your mind, body, and a ready will to share it.

Then the Word will be near you, in your mouth and heart. The Word of the Lord is the precious talent that redeems you.

—*St. Ambrose, brother of St. Marcellina*

PRAYER.   *St. Marcellina, help me to imitate you by putting the needs of others first.*

JULY 18   St. Camillus de Lellis +1614

 EITHER this man nor his parents sinned, but it happened so that the works of God might be revealed in him. We must do the works of Him Who sent Me while it is still day. —Jn 9:3-4

REFLECTION. The true apostolic life consists in not giving oneself excess rest or repose.

—*St. Camillus*

PRAYER. *St. Camillus, through your illnesses you learned to serve the sick and dying. Let me, regardless of my state of health, seek to help those who are sick, suffering, and dying.*

JULY 19   St. Macrina the Younger +379*

 WAS entrusted to Your care from birth; from my mother's womb, You have been my God. —Ps 22:11

REFLECTION. Courage and confidence are our weapons to divert the enemy's surprise attacks.

Hope and patience are the staffs to lean on when we are worn out by worldly trials.

—*St. Gregory of Nyssa, brother of St. Macrina*

PRAYER. *St. Macrina, may I encourage others in my life by my Christian example.*

St. Elijah +Ninth Century BC.*   JULY 20

 HAVE been very zealous for the Lord, the God of hosts . . . and they are seeking my life, to take it away.   —1 Ki 19:10

REFLECTION.   O Lord, God of Abraham, Isaac, and Israel, let it be known this day that You are God in Israel, and that I am Your servant, and that I have done all these things at Your command.   —St. Elijah

PRAYER.   *St. Elijah, just as you cared only for the will of God, and not the opinions of people, help me also to do God's will always.*

St. Lawrence of Brindisi +1619   JULY 21

 HE Lord is my light and my salvation; whom should I fear? The Lord is the stronghold of my life; of whom should I be afraid?   —Ps 27:1

REFLECTION.   The food that is necessary for living this life is the grace of the Holy Spirit and the love of God.

But grace and love are nothing without faith, since without faith it is impossible to please God.   —St. Lawrence

PRAYER.   *St. Lawrence, you used your intellect to inspire faith. Help me to use my mind and my words to encourage faith in others.*

JULY 22　St. Mary Magdalene +First Century

O not be alarmed; you are looking for Jesus of Nazareth, Who was crucified. He has been raised . . . He is going ahead of you to Galilee; there you will see Him.

—Mk 16:6-7

REFLECTION.　They have taken away my Lord and I do not know where they have laid Him.

Rabbouni! I have seen the Lord!

—*St. Mary Magdalene*

PRAYER.　*St. Mary Magdalene, you are the first one Jesus appeared to after He rose. Help me to be worthy to carry the message of Jesus's life, death, and resurrection.*

JULY 23　St. Bridget +1373

NE of the soldiers thrust a lance into His side, and immediately a flow of blood and water came forth. —Jn 19:34

REFLECTION.　Blessed may You be, my Lord Jesus Christ. For our salvation You allowed Your side and heart to be pierced with a lance and from Your side water and Your precious blood flowed.　　　　—*St. Bridget*

PRAYER.　*St. Bridget, may my passion for Christ's passion be like yours.*

St. Boris and St. Gleb +1015*　　　JULY 24

 LOOK upon me, O Lord, my God, and answer me; enlighten my eyes, lest I sleep in death, lest my enemy say, "I have defeated him." —Ps 13:4-5

REFLECTION. I am in your hands. I don't know why I have to die, but God knows. Who would ask brother to kill brother?

I am betrayed, O Lord, as You Yourself were. —*St. Gleb*

PRAYER. *Sts. Boris and Gleb, you were both willing to die rather than to kill. Help me promote peace through my words and actions.*

St. James +44　　　JULY 25

 KING Herod persecuted certain members of the church. He had James, the brother of John, killed by the sword. —Acts 12:1-2

REFLECTION. "You will indeed drink My cup. But to sit at My right hand and at My left, this is not Mine to grant, but it is for those for whom it has been prepared by My Father."
—*Jesus, in response to James and John's request to sit next to Him in heaven*

PRAYER. *St. James, may I learn humility and self-sacrifice in my devotion to Jesus.*

JULY 26   **St. Anne and**
                    St. Joachim +First Century

 Y mouth is filled with Your praises as I relate Your glory all day long.

—Ps 71:8

REFLECTION. Today we give thanks for the parents of the Mother of God. They are at the very beginning of the salvation of us all.

The Lord . . . blessed the house of the righteous Joachim and Anne because of their holy daughter, Mary, Mother of God. —*Bl. Cosmas*

PRAYER. *Sts. Anne and Joachim, remind me to bless all of my "parents" in faith.*

JULY 27   **St. Pantaleon** +c. 305*

 HIS is My commandment: Love one another as I have loved you.

—Jn 15:12

REFLECTION. Follow the Lord's example, strong and steadfast in faith, loving one another.

United in truth, display the Lord's own gentleness with one another, and look down on no one. If you can do good, do not put it off.

—*St. Polycarp*

PRAYER. *St. Pantaleon, may your compassion in healing the poor teach me generosity.*

St. Samson of Dol +565* **JULY 28**

MEANWHILE, the Church throughout Judea, Galilee, and Samaria enjoyed peace, building up strength.

—Acts 9:31a

REFLECTION. It is good and precious in the Lord's sight when all of Christ's people work together.

When we all follow God's Spirit, we rejoice not only over the things we do on our own but also the things others do. —*St. Leo I*

PRAYER. *St. Samson, in your humility, you allowed others to teach you. Help me to learn from my fellow Christians.*

St. Martha +First Century **JULY 29**

JESUS said to her, "I am the resurrection and the life. Whoever believes in Me, even though he dies, will live." —Jn 11:25-26

REFLECTION. Lord, if You had been here, my brother would not have died. But even now I know that God will grant You whatever You ask of Him.

I believe that You are the Christ, the Son of God, the One who is to come into the world.

—*St. Martha*

PRAYER. *St. Martha, your faith and pragmatism inspire me to take action based on my faith. Give me the courage to act!*

JULY 30   St. Peter Chrysologus +c. 450

 ND the Word became flesh and dwelt among us. And we saw His glory, . . . the Father's only Son, full of grace and peace. —Jn 1:14

REFLECTION. If the world cannot contain God, how could the limited gaze of a human person contain Him? But love is not based on what will be, nor by what is possible.

Love knows nothing of this law; it has no rule, it knows no bounds. —St. Peter

PRAYER. *St. Peter, just as your sermons inspired multitudes, may I listen to those who speak by the Spirit of God.*

JULY 31   St. Ignatius of Loyola +1556

 E cried out, "Father, into Your hands I commend My Spirit." And with these words, He breathed His last. —Lk 23:46

REFLECTION. Lord, I freely yield all my freedom to You. Take my memory, my intellect, and my entire will. You have given me everything I am or have; I give it all back to You to stand under Your will alone.

Your love and your grace are enough for me. —St. Ignatius

PRAYER. *St. Ignatius, help me to follow you in surrendering myself entirely to Jesus.*

St. Alphonsus Liguori +1787   AUG. 1

 LL the ends of the earth will remember and turn to the Lord. All the families of the nations will bow low before Him.

—Ps 22:28

REFLECTION. All holiness and perfection of life resides in our love for Jesus Christ, Who is our redeemer and our supreme good.

Has not God won for Himself a claim on all our love? From all eternity He has loved us.

—*St. Alphonsus*

PRAYER. *St. Alphonsus, remind me that all of my love for God is nothing next to His love for me; and so I must love Him even more!*

St. Eusebius of Vercelli +371   AUG. 2

 HERE is one God, and . . . one Mediator between God and man, Christ Jesus, Himself a man, Who gave Himself as a ransom for all.   —1 Tim 2:5-6

REFLECTION. I rejoice . . . in your good works, which are not limited to your surroundings but spread far and wide.

I want not only to care for all of you, but also to give my life for your well-being.

—*St. Eusebius*

PRAYER. *St. Eusebius, you endured shame and exile for your faith; help me to pray for those who mock my faith.*

113

AUG. 3 Blessed Augustine Gazotich +1323*

Y heart is steadfast, O God, my heart is steadfast. I will sing and chant Your praise; awake my soul! —Ps 108:2

REFLECTION. Faith has to do with things that are not seen and hope with things that are not at hand. —*St. Thomas Aquinas*

PRAYER. *Blessed Augustine, through your constant hope you renewed the clergy. Help me to hope in the Lord's renewal of my spirit.*

AUG. 4 St. John Vianney +1859

MMEDIATELY, the father of the child cried out, "I do believe! Help my unbelief!" —Mk 9:24

REFLECTION. We should not have been allowed to pray, but God, in His goodness, let us speak with Him.

Our prayer expands the heart and makes it capable of loving God. Prayer is a foretaste of heaven. —*St. John Vianney*

PRAYER. *St. John Vianney, your zeal helped you overcome obstacles. Let me never be indifferent to prayer's power.*

Dedication of St. Mary Major   AUG. 5
(St. Mary of the Snows) 435

 HE angel came to her and said, "Hail full of grace! The Lord is with you."

—Lk 1:28

REFLECTION.   By Paul's preaching the Word of Truth, many were born again; but Mary, . . . gave birth to the Word himself.

I do indeed praise the ministry . . . of Paul; but far more do I admire and venerate that mystery of generation in Mary.   —*Bl. Guerric of Igny*

PRAYER.   *Mary, protect and guide us in the midst of personal and global troubles.*

The Holy Transfiguration   AUG. 6

 ROM the cloud came a Voice that said, "This is My Son, the Beloved; listen to Him!"

—Lk 9:35

REFLECTION.   On Mount Tabor, Jesus revealed a heavenly mystery to His disciples.

To remove from their hearts any doubt concerning the kingdom and to confirm their faith in the future, He gave them on Mount Tabor a vision of His glory, a foreshadowing of the kingdom of heaven.   —*St. Anastasius of Sinai*

PRAYER.   *Beloved Jesus, let the brilliant light of Your Transfiguration blind me to all doubt.*

AUG. 7 St. Cajetan +1547

Y sheep listen to My voice. I know them, and they follow Me. I give them eternal life and they will never perish.
—Jn 10:27-28

REFLECTION. We are pilgrims in this world, on a journey to our true home in heaven.

While on earth we should strive to gain eternal life by obeying Jesus and remaining united with Him. —*St. Cajetan*

PRAYER. *St. Cajetan, help me avoid pride and embrace obedience to the Lord.*

AUG. 8 St. Dominic +1221

AITH comes through what is heard, and what is heard comes through the word of Christ. And so I ask, "Have they not heard?"
—Rom 10:17-18

REFLECTION. For a long time I have appealed to you in vain, with gentleness, preaching, praying, and weeping. According to the proverb of my country, "Where blessing can accomplish nothing, blows may prevail."

Must blows prevail where gentleness and blessings have been powerless? —*St. Dominic*

PRAYER. *St. Dominic, founder of the powerful preaching order, the Dominicans, help me to choose words over blows.*

St. Teresa Benedicta of the Cross (Edith Stein) +1942

HEN Thomas said to his fellow disciples, "Let us also go so that we may die with Him." —Jn 11:16

REFLECTION. Because she was Jewish, Edith Stein was taken with other Catholics and Jews to the concentration camp in Auschwitz, where she died in the gas chambers.

A few days before her deportation (she) refused to be rescued: "Do not do it! Why should I be spared?" —*Pope John Paul II*

PRAYER. *St. Teresa, let your extraordinary courage inspire me to follow Jesus all the way to the cross.*

St. Lawrence +258

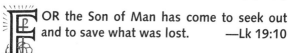OR the Son of Man has come to seek out and to save what was lost. —Lk 19:10

REFLECTION. I will show you a valuable part (of the Church). But give me some time to put things in order and make an inventory.

These (pointing to the many poor, disabled, orphaned, widowed people he had gathered) are the treasure of the Church. —*St. Lawrence*

PRAYER. *St. Lawrence, remind me that the Church is only as strong as its weakest members.*

AUG. 11   St. Clare of Assisi +1253

O not store up treasures for yourselves on earth . . . rather store up treasure for yourselves in heaven. —Mt 6:19-20

REFLECTION. O most gentle Jesus, having redeemed me by baptism from original sin, so now by Your Precious Blood deliver me from all evils, past, present and to come.

May I be strong and steadfast in good works and persevering in Your service. —*St. Clare*

PRAYER. *St. Clare, lead me away from worldly pursuits to serve Christ in the poor.*

AUG. 12   St. Euplius +304*

AM not ashamed of the gospel, since it is the power of God that offers salvation to everyone who has faith—to Jews first, and then to Gentiles as well. —Rom 1:16

REFLECTION. "If anyone will come after Me, let him deny himself and take up his cross and follow Me." It is the law of my Lord, which has been delivered to me by Jesus Christ, the Son of the living God.

I repeat what I said before: I am a Christian and I read the Sacred Scriptures. —*St. Euplius*

PRAYER. *St. Euplius, let your love for the Gospels inspire me to read them carefully in the Spirit.*

St. Pontian and
St. Hippolytus +c. 236

HEN the Son of Man comes in His glory, and all the angels with Him, then He will sit on the throne of His glory. —Mt 25:31

REFLECTION. Christ, like a well-trained physician, knows the failings of men. He loves to turn the sinful back to His own true way.

To those of pure eye and holy heart, who knock at the door, He opens immediately.

—*St. Hippolytus*

PRAYER. *Sts. Pontian and Hippolytus, remind me to avoid judging others.*

St. Maximilian Mary Kolbe +1941 AUG. 14

HEY) joined in the mockery, saying, "He saved others, but He cannot save Himself." —Mk 15:31

REFLECTION. I prayed to Our Lady to tell me what would happen. She appeared, holding in her hands two crowns, one white, one red. She asked if I would like to have them—one was for purity, the other for martyrdom.

I said, "I choose both." —*St. Maximilian*

PRAYER. *St. Maximilian, you gave your life for another. Help me to give a small part of myself for another every day.*

AUG. 15   **Assumption of the Blessed Virgin**

HE time came for her to have her Child, and she gave birth to her firstborn Son.
—Lk 2:6-7

REFLECTION. It was truly fitting that she should be taken up into heaven and not lie in the grave till Christ's second coming.

Who could believe that God would repay His Mother for elements of His human Body, by allowing the flesh and blood from which it was taken to decay in the grave?

—*Cardinal Newman*

PRAYER. *Blessed Mother, at my death guide me gently into the kingdom of your Son.*

AUG. 16   **St. Stephen of Hungary** +1038

E of one mind, sympathetic, filled with love for one another, and humble.
—1 Pet 3:8

REFLECTION. Be patient with everyone, not only with the powerful, but also with the weak.

Be humble in this life that God may raise you up in the next. Be truly moderate, and do not punish anyone inordinately.   —*St. Stephen*

PRAYER. *Stephen, king and saint, help me use what power I have to advance the will of God.*

St. Clare of Montefalco +1308*   **AUG. 17**

 FFER to God a sacrifice of thanksgiving and fulfill your vows to the Most High. Then if you cry out to Me in time of trouble, I will rescue you and you will honor Me.   —Ps 50:14-15

REFLECTION. Who teaches the soul, if not God? There is no better instruction for life than that which comes from God.

If God did not protect me, I would be the greatest sinner in the world.   *—St. Clare*

PRAYER. *St. Clare, help me to recognize my ignorance and my failings and turn to God for instruction, forgiveness, and protection.*

St. Jane Frances de Chantal +1641 **AUG. 18**

 Y God, my God, why have You forsaken me? Why have you paid no heed to my call for help?   —Ps 22:2

REFLECTION. She was full of faith, yet all her life was tortured by thoughts against it. She suffered such interior trials that . . . her mind was so filled with . . . temptations.

But for all that torment her face never lost its serenity, nor did she ever become lax in the fidelity God asked of her.   *—St. Vincent de Paul*

PRAYER. *St. Jane Frances, help me through times of doubt and spiritual dryness.*

AUG. 19   St. John Eudes +1680

HOEVER abides in Me, and I in him, will bear much fruit. —Jn 15:5

REFLECTION. Our . . . main concern must be to form Jesus in ourselves, to make His spirit, His devotion, His affections, His desires, and His disposition live and reign in us.

All our spiritual practices should be directed to this end. It is the work which God has given us to do. —*St. John*

PRAYER. *St. John, let me strive to be more like Jesus my Savior, day by day.*

AUG. 20   St. Bernard +1153

ND why am I so greatly favored that the mother of my Lord should visit me? —Lk 1:43

REFLECTION. In dangers, doubts, and difficulties, call upon Mary. Let her name be on your lips, and always in your heart.

So that you may secure the assistance of her prayers, do not neglect to walk in her footsteps. —*St. Bernard*

PRAYER. *St. Bernard, you enlivened the twelfth century Church. Help me to enliven the commitment of today's Church.*

St. Pius X +1914   AUG. 21

 ET the least person in the Kingdom of Heaven is greater than he.

—Mt 11:11

REFLECTION.   I was born poor, I lived poor, I will die poor.

This is the last affliction that the Lord will visit on me. I would gladly give my life to save my poor children from this ghastly scourge.

—*St. Pius X*

PRAYER.   *St. Pius, you preferred death to the suffering of your flock in WWI. Grant me the empathy that lets me feel the pain of others.*

Queenship of Mary   AUG. 22

 OR He has looked with favor on the lowliness of His servant; henceforth all generations will call me blessed.   —Lk 1:48

REFLECTION.   Because of the honor due her Son, it was indeed fitting for the Virgin Mother to have first ruled upon earth and then be raised up to heaven in glory.

Preserved in both flesh and spirit she bestowed healing on bodies and souls.

—*St. Amadeus of Lausanne*

PRAYER.   *Mary, Queen and Mother, rule over me gently and lead me onto the path of righteousness.*

EJOICE insofar as you are sharing in the suffering of Christ, so that your joy will be without limit when His glory is revealed.   —1 Pet 4:13

REFLECTION.   If only those on earth would learn how great it is to possess divine grace, how beautiful, how noble, how precious.

How many riches it possesses within itself, how many joys and delights!   —*St. Rose*

PRAYER.   *St. Rose, you proclaimed the power of grace in affliction. May I find in my suffering the opportunity for grace.*

AUG. 24   St. Bartholomew +First Century

HOEVER acknowledges Me before men, the Son of Man will also acknowledge before the angels of God.   —Lk 12:8

REFLECTION.   Like Christ Himself, the Apostles were unceasingly bent upon bearing witness to the truth of God.

With a firm faith they held that the Gospel is indeed the power of God unto salvation for all who believe . . . they followed the example of the gentleness and respectfulness of Christ.
          —*Declaration on Religious Freedom, 11*

PRAYER.   *St. Bartholomew, help me to spread the Gospel as you did.*

St. Louis +1270　　　　　　　　AUG. 25

 HEN you host a dinner, do not invite
. . . wealthy neighbors. Rather . . . invite the poor, the crippled, the lame,
and the blind.　　　　—Lk 14:12-13

REFLECTION.　Be kind to the poor, the unfor-
tunate, and the afflicted. Help and console
them as much as you can. Thank God for all
the blessings He has bestowed upon you.

Always side with the poor rather than with
the rich until you are certain of the truth.

—*St. Louis*

PRAYER.　*St. Louis, lead me to advocate for
the poor and disenfranchised.*

St. Melchizedek +Abrahamic Era*　　AUG. 26

 HE Lord has sworn, and He will not re-
tract His oath: "You are a priest forever
according to the order of Melchizedek."
　　　　—Ps 110:4

REFLECTION.　Blessed be Abram by God Most
High, Maker of heaven and earth; and blessed
be God Most High, who has delivered your
enemies into your hand.　—*St. Melchizedek*

PRAYER.　*St. Melchizedek, in blessing Abraham, you prophesied Jesus, the Messiah. Help
me to meditate on the many Old Testament
prophecies about Jesus.*

AUG. 27   St. Monica +387

 I HAVE always striven to preach the gospel of Christ where the name of Christ is not known. —Rom 15:20

REFLECTION. Augustine, my son . . . I had one reason for wanting to live: to see you become a Catholic Christian before I died.

God has lavished His gifts on me . . . for I know that you have even renounced earthly happiness to be His servant. —St. Monica

PRAYER. *St. Monica, your prayers converted your son. Convert me to selflessness.*

AUG. 28   St. Augustine +430

 YOU shall love the Lord your God with all your heart, and with all your soul, and with all your strength, and with all your mind. —Lk 10:27

REFLECTION. My love of You, O Lord, is not some vague feeling: it is positive and certain. Your word pierced my heart and from that moment I loved you.

Besides this, all about me, heaven and earth and all that they contain proclaim that I should love you. —St. Augustine

PRAYER. *St. Augustine, lead me to love the Lord fervently and to act according to that love.*

Martyrdom of
St. John the Baptist +First Century

ND as he watched Jesus walk by (John) exclaimed, "Look, here is the Lamb of God!" —Jn 1:36

REFLECTION. I am baptizing you with water, for repentance, but the One who is coming after me is mightier than I. I am not worthy to carry His sandals.

He will baptize you with the Holy Spirit and fire. —*St. John the Baptist*

PRAYER. *St. John the Baptist, help me to be cleansed of my sins so that I may help prepare the way of the Lord.*

St. Pammachius +410*

OT to us. O Lord, not to us, but to Your name give glory because of Your kindness and faithfulness. —Ps 115:1

REFLECTION. God created us with free will, and we aren't forced to choose to be righteous or to be wicked.

But God perfects us in good works. For we don't reach perfection because of our will . . . but because God helps us to reach the goal. —*St. Jerome*

PRAYER. *St. Pammachius, your friendship with St. Jerome required sacrifice. May my free will lead me to kindness.*

AUG. 31 — St. Aristedes +c. 150*

ITH great power, the apostles bore witness to the resurrection of the Lord Jesus, and they were all greatly respected. —Acts 4:33

REFLECTION. Aristedes a faithful disciple of our religion, has left an Apology of the Faith dedicated to Hadrian. His writing has also been kept by many, even to the present time.

—*St. Eusebius*

PRAYER. *St. Aristedes, you used your great learning to defend and promote the early Church. Help me to work always to advance the Gospels.*

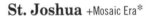

SEPT. 1 — St. Joshua +Mosaic Era*

OW therefore, revere the Lord and serve him in sincerity and in faithfulness. —Jos 24:14

REFLECTION. Your actions do not witness to having chosen the Lord, to serve Him.

Put away the foreign gods that are among you, and incline your hearts to the Lord, the God of Israel. —*St. Joshua*

PRAYER. *St. Joshua, God chose you to lead after Moses. Despite my unworthiness may I strive to lead people to Him.*

Bl. Solomon Le Clerq +1792*   SEPT.2

 OR the Father Himself loves you because you have loved Me and have come to believe that I came from God.   —Jn 16:27

REFLECTION.   Love attracts all the good there is in heaven, in the angels and the saints and all the sufferings of the martyrs.

Love draws . . . all the good that is contained in all the creatures in heaven and on earth.   —Johannes Tauler

PRAYER.   *Bl. Solomon you died for your love of Christ. Increase my love for the Lord.*

St. Gregory the Great +604   SEPT. 3

 F I tell you about earthly things and you do not believe, how will you believe when I speak to you about heavenly things?
    —Jn 3:12

REFLECTION.   Perhaps it is not as difficult for someone to part with material things as it is to part with himself.

To renounce what one has is a small thing; but to renounce what one is, that is asking a lot.   —St. Gregory

PRAYER.   *St. Gregory, let me renounce any part of me that is not focused on God.*

SEPT. 4 St. Rosalia +1160*

O not be concerned about your life and what you will have . . . Surely life is more than food and the body is more than clothing. —Mt 6:25

REFLECTION. I, Rosalia, daughter of Sinibald, Lord of Roses and Quisquina, have taken the resolution to live in this cave for the love of my Lord, Jesus Christ. —*St. Rosalia*

PRAYER. *St. Rosalia, you rejected the world to live for Jesus. Remind me to put aside solitary time to meditate on the Lord and welcome Him into my heart.*

SEPT. 5 Bl. Teresa of Calcutta +1997*

HE command I give you is this: love one another. —Jn 15:17

REFLECTION. Because we cannot see God, we cannot yet express our love to Him face to face.

But for our neighbor who we can see, we can do what we would love to do for Jesus if He were visible. Joy is a net of love by which we can capture souls. —*Bl. Teresa*

PRAYER. *Mother Teresa, may I see Jesus in everyone I meet.*

Bl. Bertrand of Garrigues +c. 1230* **SEP. 6**

 O You, O Lord, I will offer praise in song. I will walk in the path of blamelessness; when will You come to me?
—Ps 101:1-2

REFLECTION. The one who governs his passions is master of the world. We must either command them, or be a slave to them.

It is better to be a hammer than an anvil.
—*St. Dominic*

PRAYER. *Bl. Bertrand, you imitated your mentor, St. Dominic, by choosing words over war. Help me to wage peace in the name of Jesus.*

St. Cloud +560* **SEP. 7**

 HE future bodes well for him who is generous in helping those in need and who conducts his affairs with justice.
—Ps 112:5

REFLECTION. Don't be discouraged if you don't see the good you do. Most of the time people grow through their hidden sacrifices, rather than a busy public ministry.

Above all, let us try to lay aside our own ego.
—*Venerable Thecla Merlo*

PRAYER. *St. Cloud, you renounced ambition and violence to toil for the Lord. May I be ruled by faith, not ego.*

SEPT. 8   The Nativity of Mary

 EHOLD the virgin shall conceive and give birth to a son, and they shall name Him Emmanuel. —Isa 7:14

REFLECTION. Today, the Virgin is born, nurtured, and prepared for her role as Mother of God, Who is the universal King of the ages.

It is appropriate that we celebrate this mystery since it signified to us a double grace.

—*St. Andrew of Crete*

PRAYER. *Mary, light of your parents' old age, joy of the ages, I pray for the welfare of all mothers and their children.*

SEPT. 9   St. Peter Claver +1654

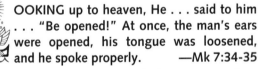 OOKING up to heaven, He . . . said to him . . . "Be opened!" At once, the man's ears were opened, his tongue was loosened, and he spoke properly. —Mk 7:34-35

REFLECTION. The joy in their eyes as they watched us was wonderful to see. This is how we communicate with them, not with words but with gestures and actions.

We taught them about baptism . . . the wonderful effects of the sacrament. —*St. Peter*

PRAYER. *St. Peter, you called yourself "slave of the blacks." Lead me to assist people of color and others in need.*

St. Nicholas of Tolentine +1305* SEPT. 10

 OLY Father, protect by the power of Your Name those You have given Me, so that they may be one, even as We are One. —Jn 17:11

REFLECTION. Almighty God can complete anyone He pleases. But God desires that we depend on each other, and what anyone does not have in himself, he finds in the other.

Thus, humility is preserved, love increased, and unity realized. —St. Aelred

PRAYER. *St. Nicholas, let me imitate you in your patience, love, and humility.*

St. John Gabriel Perboyre +1840* SEPT. 11

 OR You are my help, and in the shadow of Your wings I rejoice. My soul clings tightly to You. —Ps 63:8-9

REFLECTION. There is a love like a small oil lamp that goes out when the oil is used. But there is love like a spring rushing from the earth, never to be consumed.

The first is human; the second is Divine and has God as its source. —St. Isaak of Syria

PRAYER. *St. John, you were martyred after protecting orphans. Lead me to volunteer with a group that helps children.*

SEPT. 12 The Most Holy Name of Mary

HE angel Gabriel was sent by God . . . to a virgin. The virgin's name was Mary.
—Lk 1:26-27

REFLECTION. With your hand in hers, you will never falter. With her protecting you, you will have no fear. Her kindness will always be with you.

Then you will know from your own experience how true it is that "the Virgin's name was Mary." —*St. Bernard of Clairvaux*

PRAYER. *Mary, whenever I am in danger, let me call upon your name; help me!*

SEPT. 13 St. John Chrysostom +407

HE true light that enlightens everyone was coming into the world.
—Jn 1:9

REFLECTION. Witnessing to others is what it means to be a Christian.

It would be easier for the sun to stop shining and giving forth heat than for a Christian not to send forth light; easier for the light to be darkness than for this to be so. —*St. John*

PRAYER. *St. John, you were exiled for honest witnessing. Let my Christian light shine forth, no matter the risk.*

Exaltation of the Holy Cross   SEPT. 14

HEN Jesus said, "Father, forgive them, for they do not know what they are doing."   —Lk 23:34

REFLECTION.   How splendid the cross of Christ! It brings life, not death; light, not darkness; Paradise, not its loss.

It is the wood on which the Lord, like a noble soldier, was wounded in hands and feet and side, but through them healed our wounds.   —*Theodore of Studios*

PRAYER.   *Jesus, by Your cross, You redeemed the world. I praise and thank You, Lord!*

Our Lady of Sorrows   SEPT. 15

OME, all who pass by the way, look and see whether there is any suffering like my suffering.   —Lam 1:12

REFLECTION.   At the cross her station keeping, / Stood the mournful mother weeping, / Close to Jesus to the last.

Through her heart, His sorrow sharing, / All His bitter anguish bearing, / Now at length the sword has passed.   —*Stabat Mater*

PRAYER.   *Mother of Jesus, your suffering is incomprehensible. Help me to be mindful of your pain.*

135

SEPT. 16   St. Cornelius +252 and St. Cyprian +258

 PRAY not only on behalf of these, but also for those who through their word will come to believe in Me.   —Jn 17:20

REFLECTION.   When we pray, we pray not for one person but for all, because we are all one.

God, the Master of peace and harmony, desires that we should pray for all even as He Himself bore us all.   —St. Cyprian

PRAYER.   *Sts. Cornelius and Cyprian, teach me to be generous and unifying in my prayers.*

SEPT. 17   St. Robert Bellarmine +1621

 LOVE You, O Lord, my strength, O Lord, my rock, my fortress, my deliverer.   —Ps 18:2

REFLECTION.   It is . . . that first and greatest commandment: "You shall love the Lord your God with all your heart."

What is easier, sweeter, more pleasant, than to love goodness, beauty and love, the fullness of which You are, O Lord my God?

    —St. Robert

PRAYER.   *St. Robert, your great learning and study drew you closer to God. Let me find God in the Scriptures.*

St. Joseph of Cupertino +1663* SEPT. 18

T O You, O Lord, I lift up my soul; in You, O my God, I trust. —Ps 25:1-2

REFLECTION. My mother (Mary) is very unusual; if I bring her flowers, she says she does not want them; if I bring her cherries, she will not take them.

When I ask her what she wants, she responds: "I desire your heart, for I live on hearts."

—St. Joseph

PRAYER. *St. Joseph, your simplicity and reputation for levitation reminds me to lift my own heart and spirit up to God.*

St. Januarius (Gennaro) +305 SEPT. 19

 HE thought, "If I simply touch His clothing, I shall be made well." And . . . she was healed. —Mk 5:28-29

REFLECTION. A dark mass that fills a hermetically sealed four-inch glass container halfway, and is preserved in a double reliquary in the Naples cathedral as the blood of St. Januarius, liquifies 18 times each year.

The phenomenon eludes natural explanation. —*Catholic Encyclopedia*

PRAYER. *St. Januarius, let me embrace miracles, both small and large.*

137

SEPT. 20 Sts. Andrew Kim Taegon, Paul Chong Hasang, and Companions +1838-1867

Y heart is filled with anguish, and I am beset by the terrors of death. Fear and trembling overpower me. —Ps 55:5-6

REFLECTION. The Korean Church is unique because it was founded by laypeople only. This young Church, so strong in faith, withstood wave after wave of intense persecution.

In less than a century, it could boast of 10,000 martyrs. —*Pope John Paul II*

PRAYER. *Sts. Andrew, Paul and Companions, inspire me to learn about the Church in troubled nations.*

SEPT. 21 St. Matthew +First Century

ESUS . . . saw a man named Matthew sitting at the tax booth; and He said to him, "Follow Me." And he got up and followed Him. —Mt 9:9

REFLECTION. As He sat at dinner . . . many tax collectors and sinners came and were sitting with Him. When the Pharisees saw this, they said to His disciples, "Why does your Teacher eat with tax collectors and sinners?"

But He said, ". . . I have come to call not the righteous, but sinners." —*St. Matthew*

PRAYER. *St. Matthew, lead me to speak freely and joyfully of Jesus.*

St. Emmerammus +c. 690*   SEPT. 22

ATHER, if You are willing, take this cup from Me. Yet not My will but Yours be done. —Lk 22:42

REFLECTION. You surely will yet save me! Your will shall be done. I will follow Your plan and labor to form my will to Yours.

May Your will, O my God, be forever done and always in perfection. —*St. Francis de Sales*

PRAYER. *St. Emmerammus, allow me to be led in the direction God chooses for me.*

St. Pio of Pietrelcina +1968   SEPT. 23

HEN Jesus entered the temple and drove out all those whom He found buying and selling there. —Mt 21:12

REFLECTION. Regard as free not those who are free from their status, but those who are free in their life and disposition.

Freedom and blessedness of the soul are the result of true purity and contempt of temporal things. —*St. Anthony the Great*

PRAYER. *Padre Pio, by suffering the Stigmata and rejecting worldly life, you lead me to meditate on Jesus' wounds.*

139

SEPT. 24 St. Pacific of San Severino +1721*

GROAN as I think of God; my spirit grows faint as I meditate on Him. —Ps 77:4

REFLECTION. My divine Master showed me that my soul was the blank canvas on which He wished to paint all the details of His life of suffering, totally spent in love and poverty, solitude, silence and sacrifice.

But that will only be if I suffer for Him.
—*St. Margaret Mary Alacoque*

PRAYER. *St. Pacific, help me find redemption in suffering for Jesus as you did.*

SEPT. 25 St. Cleophas +First Century*

ESUS Himself came near and went with them, but their eyes were kept from recognizing Him. —Lk 24:15-16

REFLECTION. Are you the only stranger in Jerusalem who does not know the things that have taken place in these days?

Moreover, some women of our group . . . told us that they had seen a vision of angels who said that He was alive. —*St. Cleophas*

PRAYER. *St. Cleophas, help me recognize Jesus in the blessing of the Eucharist, just as you did.*

St. Gideon +Era of the Hebrew Judges*   **SEPT. 26**

 HE angel of the Lord . . . said to (Gideon), "The Lord is with you, you mighty warrior."   —Jdg 6:12

REFLECTION. Do not leave this place until I come and bring you my gift and set it before You.

Help me, Lord God! For I have seen the angel of the Lord face to face.   *—St. Gideon*

PRAYER. *St. Gideon, help me to seek God's favor so that I may be able to heed His call and do His will.*

———

St. Vincent de Paul +1660   **SEPT. 27**

HE poor you will always have with you, but you will not always have Me.

    —Jn 12:8

REFLECTION. We prefer to serve the poor and to offer such service as quickly as possible.

If a needy person requires your help during prayer time, do whatever has to be done with peace of mind. Offer the work to God as your prayer.   *—St. Vincent de Paul*

PRAYER. *St. Vincent, let me pray in and through my service to the poor.*

SEPT. 28 Sts. Lawrence Ruiz
and Companions +1633-37

E was prophesying that Jesus was to die
. . . not for the nation alone but to gather
into one the dispersed children of God.
—Jn 11:51-52

REFLECTION. I shall never renounce my faith
because I am a Christian, and I shall die for
God, and for Him I would give my life again
and again if I could.

And so, do with me as you please.

—*St. Lawrence*

PRAYER. *St. Lawrence, help me to act as if
each day is a new life I have to give for God.*

SEPT. 29 Sts. Michael, Gabriel,
Raphael, Archangels

ABRIEL . . . came to me in swift flight
. . . and said to me, "Daniel, I have now
come out to give you wisdom and understanding." —Dan 9:21-22

REFLECTION. Those holy spirits of heaven . . .
can only be called Angels when they deliver a
message.

Moreover . . . those who announce messages of supreme importance are called
"Archangels." —*St. Gregory the Great*

PRAYER. *Archangels of God, I am in awe of
your powers and functions. Remind me to be
ever receptive of God's messages.*

St. Jerome +420   SEP. 30

 JUST as one man's transgression brought condemnation for all, so one Man's righteous act resulted in justification and life for all.   —Rom 5:18

REFLECTION. The land of the living is the place where the goodness of the Lord has been prepared for the saints and the meek.

The first Adam had lost it and the second Adam found it again, or rather . . . the second has restored it.   —*St. Jerome*

PRAYER. *St. Jerome, help me to always seek the land of the living restored by Jesus.*

St. Thérèse of the Child Jesus +1897 OCT. 1

 THE greatest among you should be like the youngest, and the leader must be like the one who serves.   —Lk 22:26

REFLECTION. When a Sister asks me for anything, I do it right away and then give it no further thought.

When I pray for my brother missionaries, I don't offer my sufferings. I say simply, My God, give them everything I desire for myself.

     —*St. Thérèse*

PRAYER. *St. Thérèse, your simplicity and unshakable faith through suffering teach me humility.*

OCT. 2   The Guardian Angels

 EE that you do not despise one of these little ones for I say to you that their Angels in heaven continually gaze upon the face of my heavenly Father. —Mt 18:10

REFLECTION. Even though we are children and have a very long and dangerous way to go, with such guardians what have we to fear?

They who care for us in all our ways cannot be destroyed or led astray, much less lead us astray. —*St. Bernard of Clairvaux*

PRAYER. *Guardian Angel, protect and lead me on the path to Jesus.*

OCT. 3   St. Gerard of Brogne +959*

 HE stone that the builders rejected has become the cornerstone; by the Lord has this been done, and it is wonderful in our eyes. —Mt 21:42

REFLECTION. When evil thoughts come into one's heart, (it is best) to strike them at once on the rock of Christ and to confess them to one's spiritual advisor.

And never to despair of God's mercy.

—*St. Benedict*

PRAYER. *St. Gerard, by restoring the monasteries, you nurtured faith. Let me nurture faith from its first spark.*

St. Francis of Assisi +1226   OCT. 4

 ESUS . . . said to them, "Take nothing for the journey, neither walking staff, nor sack, nor bread, nor money.   —Lk 9:3

REFLECTION.   Above all the gifts . . . of the Holy Spirit which Christ grants to His friends, is that of self-sacrifice and of willingly bearing discomforts for the love of Christ.

In all the other gifts of God we cannot glory, inasmuch as they are not ours, but of God.   —*St. Francis*

PRAYER.   *St. Francis, inspire me to give myself and all I have to God.*

St. Faustina Kowalska +1938*   OCT. 5

 URN to me and have mercy on me, for I am alone and afflicted.   —Ps 25:16

REFLECTION.   The Lord is gracious and merciful and rejoices in the conversion of the sinner.

Patient and generous in His mercy, He is not disturbed by human impatience, but is able to wait a long time for our repentance.

—*St. Jerome*

PRAYER.   *St. Faustina, apostle of the Divine Mercy, let me be merciful as I ask God to grant me mercy.*

145

OCT. 6   Bl. Marie Rose Durocher +1849

 N hearing this, some Pharisees who were present asked Him, "Are we blind too?" —Jn 9:40

REFLECTION. "Jesus, Mary, Joseph! Sweet Jesus, I love You."

"Your prayers are keeping me here—let me go." —*Bl. Marie Rose on her deathbed, to the sister who was attending to her*

PRAYER. *Bl. Marie, you devoted your life to the poor. Let me support—financially and prayerfully—poor students seeking an education.*

OCT. 7   Our Lady of the Rosary

 HE mother of Jesus was there, and Jesus and His disciples had also been invited. —Jn 2:1-2

REFLECTION. The Rosary sets forth the mystery of Christ.

Praying the Rosary calls for a quiet rhythm . . . helping the individual to reflect on the mysteries of the Lord's life as experienced by she who was closer to the Lord than all others. —*Pope Paul VI*

PRAYER. *Son and mother, hear my prayers as I recite the Rosary.*

St. Pelagia +c. 302* OCT. 8

LESSED are all those who take refuge in Him. —Ps 2:12

REFLECTION. What a glorious relief—to find comfort in Christ! His tears wash us and His weeping cleanses us . . .

But if you begin to doubt, you will despair. For the greater the sin, the greater the gratitude due Him. —St. Ambrose

PRAYER. *St. Pelagia, your pure faith won St. Ambrose's approval. Help me purify my faith and reject doubt.*

St. John Leonardi +1609 OCT. 9

O not be afraid, little flock, for your Father has chosen to give you the kingdom. Sell your possessions and give to those in need. —Lk 12:32

REFLECTION. Those who want to reform the world must seek the glory of God before all else.

Since He is the source of all good, they must wait and pray for His help in this difficult and necessary undertaking. —St. John

PRAYER. *St. John, help me to imitate you in trusting God in all that I undertake.*

147

OCT. 10   St. Paulinus of York +644*

JOHN answered them, "I baptize with water; but among you there is One whom you do not know." —Jn 1:26

REFLECTION. It is not proper for religion to force religion on a person, which should be one's own choice.

There is but one Baptism according to the Lord's Gospel and to the Apostle's letter.

—*Tertullian*

PRAYER. *St. Paulinus, you gently brought people to Baptism and conversion. Teach me gentleness.*

OCT. 11   St. Firminus +c. 6th Century*

INSTRUCT certain people that they are not to teach erroneous doctrines and not to concern themselves with myths and endless genealogies. —1 Tim 1:3-4

REFLECTION. The venerable priest Firminus nurtures his people with the gold of dogma.

His praise reaches through all of Italy, and his name is known outside his own country.

—*Arator, Roman poet*

PRAYER. *St. Firminus, you taught believers about the laws and history of the Church. Help me to cherish opportunities to learn.*

St. Cyprian, St. Felix c. 484* and Companions   OCT. 12

 ESUS said . . . "today you will be with Me in Paradise."

—Lk 23:43

REFLECTION. No one is saved by his own strength, but by the grace and mercy of God.

One who is not willing to go to Christ will fear death.   —*St. Cyprian*

PRAYER. *Sts. Felix and Cyprian, you were tortured and gave your lives for your beliefs. I pray that I am never tested so brutally.*

St. Gerald of Aurillac +909*   OCT. 13

 GOOD man brings forth good things from the good stored up within him.

—Mt 12:35

REFLECTION. As our Lord says, "A good tree is not able to produce bad fruit." The good tree, that is, the good heart as well as the soul on fire with charity can do nothing but good and holy works.

Be sincerely kind to every one.

—*St. Angela Merici*

PRAYER. *St. Gerald, pray with me to be a "good tree" in an often "bad" world.*

OCT. 14   St. Callistus I +222

 ET You are enthroned as the Holy One; You are the praise of Israel.   —Ps 22:4

REFLECTION. We praise and thank You, O God, through your Son, Jesus Christ, our Lord, through Whom You have enlightened us, by revealing the light that never fades.

Night is falling . . . yet . . . the evening lights do not fail us.   —*St. Hippolytus*

PRAYER. *St. Callistus, you were a light of mercy to your enemy, Hippolytus. Teach me mercy.*

OCT. 15   St. Teresa of Avila +1582

 HRIST . . . by being the first to rise from the dead . . . would proclaim light to the people and to the Gentiles.

   —Acts 26:23

REFLECTION. O Lord! All our suffering comes from not keeping our eyes on You.

We fall a thousand times and stumble and go astray because we do not keep our eyes fixed on the true Way.   —*St. Teresa*

PRAYER. *St. Teresa, your good cheer and determination inspire me to keep my eyes on Jesus Who is the Way.*

St. Gerard Majella +1755* OCT. 16

PEACE I leave with you, My peace I give to you. Not as the world gives do I give it to you. —Jn 14:27

REFLECTION. The most Blessed Sacrament is Christ made visible. The poor sick person is Christ again made visible.

Who except God can give you peace? Has the world ever been able to satisfy you?
—*St. Gerard*

PRAYER. *St. Gerard, patron of expectant mothers, help me to see all solutions in the Lord.*

St. Ignatius of Antioch +c. 107 OCT. 17

I URGE you, brethren, to listen to my words of exhortation. —Heb 13:22

REFLECTION. The Churches of God present here with me . . . comfort me in body and in soul.

I happily make my way to God, exhorting you to persevere in harmony and community prayer. —*St. Ignatius*

PRAYER. *St. Ignatius, let your fearlessness in the face of death inspire me to be fearless in life.*

151

OCT. 18 St. Luke +First Century

NO one but Luke is with me.

—2 Tim 4:11

REFLECTION. Jesus . . . had shown Himself alive to them after His passion by many demonstrations for forty days.

He had continued to appear to them and tell them about the kingdom of God . . . He had told them not to leave Jerusalem, but to wait there for what the Father had promised. *—St. Luke*

PRAYER. *St. Luke, your loyalty as both Jesus' disciple and recorder strengthens my resolve and knowledge.*

OCT. 19 St. Isaac Jogues, St. John de Brébeuf, and Companions +1642-49

HE said to them, "Go forth into the whole world and proclaim the gospel to all creation." —Mk 16:15

REFLECTION. My confidence is in God Who does not need our help to accomplish His plans.

We should give ourselves to His work and not spoil His work by our shortcomings.

—St. Isaac Jogues

PRAYER. *Saints and Martyrs, give me courage to be a missionary in my everyday life.*

152

St. Bertilla Boscardin +1922*   OCT. 20

 EHOLD, My servant, whom I have chosen, My beloved, in whom I delight.   Isa 42:1

REFLECTION.   For it is the nature of love, to love when it feels itself loved, and to love everything loved by the beloved.

Knowing the love of the Creator, the soul loves Him, and loves all things that God loves.

—*St. Catherine of Siena*

PRAYER. *St. Bertilla, help me, like you, to bring peace and healing where there is strife and pain.*

St. Hilarion +371*   OCT. 21

 KEEP the Lord always before me, for with Him at my right hand I will never fall.

—Ps 16:8

REFLECTION.   As dirt puts out a fire burning in a stove, so worldly cares and material attachments, however insignificant, destroy the warmth of the heart.   —*St. Simeon the New Theologian*

PRAYER. *St. Hilarion, your pursuit of solitude and rejection of the world remind me to spend time alone with God.*

OCT. 22   St. Donatus +c. 875*

 HE measure you give will be the measure you will receive, and you will receive more in addition. —Mk 4:24

REFLECTION. My storehouse shall be a store-house of bright testimony . . . in which plenty shall abound.

The Son of Mary, my beloved One, will bless my storehouse. His is the glory of the whole universe. —St. Bridgid

PRAYER. *St. Donatus, your biography of St. Bridgid inspires me to seek my own spiritual mentors.*

OCT. 23   St. John of Capistrano +1456

 UT as for you, man of God, you must . . . pursue righteousness, godliness, faith, love, fortitude, and gentleness.

—1 Tim 6:11

REFLECTION. Now a light does not shine for itself, but it spreads its rays and shines upon everything that comes into its view.

So it is with the glowing lives of upright and holy clerics . . . they must bring light to all who see them. —St. John

PRAYER. *St. John, I pray for the priests and religious of this day.*

St. Anthony Mary Claret +1870　　OCT. 24

IS disciples recalled the words of Scripture, "Zeal for your house will consume me."　　—Jn 2:17

REFLECTION.　The love of Christ arouses us, urges us to run and to fly, lifted on the wings of holy zeal.

The zealous man . . . labors strenuously so that God may always be better known, loved, and served.　　—*St. Anthony*

PRAYER.　*St. Anthony, writer and publisher, lead me to the word of God.*

St. Gaudentius of Brescia +410*　　OCT. 25

AKE it; this is My body." . . . "This is My blood of the covenant, which will be shed on behalf of many." —Mk 14:22-24

REFLECTION.　Creator and Lord of all things, whatever their nature, He brought forth bread from the earth and changed it into His own Body.

And as He had changed water into wine, He also changed wine into His own Blood.

—*St. Gaudentius*

PRAYER.　*St. Gaudentius, your reverence for Holy Communion inspired your flock. Lead me to inspire others to love the Eucharist.*

155

AM I not free to do as I wish with my own money? Or are you envious because I am generous?   —Mt 20:15

REFLECTION.   Those who do good things must never lose heart lest they lose their power to do good.

. . . Christ praised the widow's devotion because of her two coins. . . . For the value of our charity is based on the sincerity of our feelings.   —*St. Leo the Great*

PRAYER.   *St. Rusticus, by accepting Pope Leo the Great's encouragement, you inspire me to persevere in doing good.*

OCT. 27   **St. Odran** +c. 563*

I AM the bread of life. Whoever comes to Me will never be hungry, and whoever believes in Me will never be thirsty.   —Jn 6:35

REFLECTION.   If you thirst, drink of the fountain of life; if you are hungry, eat the bread of life.

Blessed are they who hunger for this bread and thirst for this fountain, for they will desire ever more to eat and drink.   —*St. Columba*

PRAYER.   *St. Odran, companion of St. Columba, remind me to express my faith with the work of my hands and my mind.*

St. Simon and St. Jude +First Century OCT. 28

 OWEVER, you, dear friends, must build yourselves up in your most holy faith and pray in the Holy Spirit. —Jude 20

REFLECTION. How can anyone doubt God's presence and help who has been saved from danger by His simple nod, who has crossed the sea the Savior calmed and supplied a solid road for His people? —*St. Eusebius*

PRAYER. *Sts. Simon and Jude, Apostles, let my envy of your closeness to Jesus lead me closer to Him.*

St. Narcissus +c. 222* OCT. 29

 ESUS of Nazareth was a man commended to you by God by means of miracles and portents and signs that God worked through Him. —Acts 2:22

REFLECTION. I believe that seeing miracles performed and perfected at God's command is the foundation of faith and the basis for our confidence.

Despite our difficulties there is no reason to deny our faith. —*St. Eusebius*

PRAYER. *St. Narcissus, you were praised by Eusebius for your diligence and miracle-working. Let me find strength in miracles.*

OCT. 30 — St. Marcellus +c. 298*

 HILE they were stoning Stephen, he prayed, "Lord Jesus, receive my spirit . . . Lord, do not hold this sin against them." —Acts 7:59-60

REFLECTION. The martyrs desired death, not to avoid work, but to attain their goal. And they did not fear death because they had substituted the love of their own bodies with divine and supernatural love. —*St. Catherine of Siena*

PRAYER. *St. Marcellus, I pray for all Christians who suffer and die for their faith.*

OCT. 31 — St. Wolfgang +c. 994*

 AVE you understood all this?" He asked. They answered, "Yes." —Mt 13:51

REFLECTION. We can name a thing from the knowledge we have of its nature.

The name God signifies the divine nature, for this name was given to signify that which exists above all things. —*St. Thomas Aquinas*

PRAYER. *St. Wolfgang, teacher, help me to expand my faith through education.*

All Saints   NOV. 1

FTER this in my vision, I witnessed a vast throng, that no one could count, from every nation, race, people, and tongue.   —Rev 7:9

REFLECTION.   The saints do not need praise from us; neither does our devotion add the slightest thing to them.

Clearly, if we venerate their memory it serves us, not them. But when I think of them, I feel tremendous yearning.

—*St. Bernard of Clairvaux*

PRAYER.   *I ask all saints to help make me worthy to join their ranks.*

All Souls   NOV. 2

HE Lord has made known His salvation; He has manifested His righteousness for all the nations to see.   —Ps 98:2

REFLECTION.   Eternal rest grant to them, O Lord, and let perpetual light shine upon them. May they rest in peace.   —*Prayer for the Dead*

PRAYER.   *Merciful Father, bring all the dead into Your embrace, including me and those I love at the time of our deaths.*

NOV. 3   St. Martin de Porres +1639

AY he be enthroned in God's presence forever, and may Your kindness and faithfulness watch over him. —Ps 61:8

REFLECTION. He diligently worked to redeem the guilty; lovingly he comforted the sick; he provided food, clothing and medicine for the poor; he helped laborers and slaves.

He excused the faults of others.

—*Pope John XXIII*

PRAYER. *St. Martin, help me to remain blind to skin color and status.*

NOV. 4   St. Charles Borromeo +1584

ORD, when did we see You hungry and give You something to eat, or thirsty and give You something to drink? —Mt 25:37

REFLECTION. If a small spark of God's love now burns within you, do not expose it to the wind.

In other words, avoid distractions; stay close to God. Do not waste time in useless chatter. —*St. Charles*

PRAYER. *St. Charles, your exceeding charity to the hungry inspires me to donate to soup kitchens and food pantries.*

St. Bertille +705*   **NOV. 5**

 ANY who are first will be last, and the last will be first.

—Mt 19:30

REFLECTION. The spiritually self-sufficient often make mistakes and are more difficult to correct than those who have worldly independence.

Consider yourselves, therefore, as nothing.

—*Blessed Angela of Foligno*

PRAYER. *St. Bertille, though an abbess, you were a humble servant. Teach me to lead by serving.*

St. Leonard of Noblac +c. 559*   **NOV. 6**

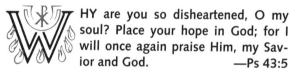 HY are you so disheartened, O my soul? Place your hope in God; for I will once again praise Him, my Savior and God.   —Ps 43:5

REFLECTION. Let us dispel all our cares by prayer and hope. But if we cannot do so completely, let us confide in God and never cease praying.

For it is better to be accused of frequent omissions than for complete neglect.

—*St. Mark the Ascetic*

PRAYER. *St. Leonard, Patron of prisoners, I pray that all prisoners be freed through prayer.*

NOV. 7   St. Engelbert +1125*

 OUR light must shine so that it can be seen . . . this will enable them to observe your good works and give praise to your Father in heaven. —Mt 5:16

REFLECTION. The everlasting God has in His wisdom foreseen from eternity the cross that He now presents to you as a gift from His all-knowing eyes, . . . warmed with loving arms and weighed with His own hands to see that it be not one inch too large and not one ounce too heavy for you. —*St. Francis de Sales*

PRAYER. *St. Engelbert, you strove tirelessly for justice as archbishop of Cologne. Help me to be a Christian in name and deed.*

NOV. 8   St. Godfrey +1115*

 UT whoever endures to the end will be saved. —Mt 24:13

REFLECTION. We must persevere if we are to gain the truth and freedom we have been hoping for.

Faith and hope are the very basis of being a Christian, but if faith and hope are to bear fruit, patience is necessary. —*St. Cyprian*

PRAYER. *St. Godfrey, just as you were steadfast, let me persevere in seeking and proclaiming the truth.*

St. Elizabeth of the Trinity +1906* **NOV. 9**

THE Advocate, the Holy Spirit, whom the Father will send in My name, will teach you everything and remind you of all that I have said to you. —Jn 14:26

REFLECTION. (A soul which) remains like a lyre under the mysterious touch of the Holy Spirit so that He may draw from it divine harmonies, knows that suffering is a string that produces still more beautiful sounds . . . that it may more delightfully move the heart of God. —*St. Elizabeth*

PRAYER. *St. Elizabeth, teach me to please the Father, Son, and Spirit.*

St. Leo the Great +461 **NOV. 10**

MY God, rescue me from the hands of the impious, from the grasp of cruel and ruthless foes. You, O Lord, are my hope. —Ps 71:4-5

REFLECTION. Every believer when renewed separates from his old origin and becomes a new person.

No longer is he a member of the family of his parents . . . but of the Savior's Who made Himself man so that we might become sons and daughters of God. —*St. Leo*

PRAYER. *St. Leo, you fought the Church's enemies. Let me oppose whatever would keep me from God.*

NOV. 11   St. Martin of Tours +397

HE word of God came to John, the son of Zechariah, in the desert. Some soldiers also asked him, "What about us? What should we do?" —Lk 3:2,14

REFLECTION. I have served you as a soldier; now let me serve Christ. Give the bounty to those who are doing the fighting.

Now I am a soldier of Christ and it is not lawful for me to fight.

—*St. Martin, refusing a war bounty*

PRAYER. *St. Martin, help me to avoid petty fights so as to become a soldier of Christ.*

NOV. 12   St. Josaphat +1623

HOEVER receives you receives Me; and whoever receives Me receives the One who sent Me. —Mt 10:40

REFLECTION. I am here as your shepherd and I would be happy to give my life for you.

I am prepared to die for the holy union, for the supremacy of St. Peter and for his successor, the Supreme Pontiff. —*St. Josaphat*

PRAYER. *St. Josaphat, teach me to sew seeds of unity, not dissension.*

St. Frances Xavier Cabrini +1917 **NOV. 13**

 DO not surrender the soul of Your dove to wild beasts; do not forget forever the life of Your poor.
—Ps 74:19

REFLECTION. Although her body was very frail, her spirit was endowed with a rare strength that, knowing the will of God, she allowed nothing to stop her from accomplishing what seemed beyond the strength of a woman. —*Pope Pius XII*

PRAYER. *St. Frances, when an act of faith seems beyond my strength, help me to reach for it anyway.*

Sts. Nicholas Tavelic and Companions +1391* **NOV. 14**

JESUS replied: "This is the work of God: to believe in the One whom He has sent."
—Jn 6:29

REFLECTION. Under no circumstances will we recant.

We are ready to die and to suffer every torture because whatever we said is holy, Catholic, and true. —*Sts. Nicholas and Companions, before being martyred*

PRAYER. *Sts. Nicholas and Companions, help me to know what is holy, Catholic, and true.*

AMEN, amen, I say to you, unless you eat the flesh of the Son of Man and drink His blood, you do not have life within you.   —Jn 6:53

REFLECTION.   "Do this in remembrance of Me."

Two things are important here. The first is, the command that we should use this Sacrament which Jesus indicated by saying, "Do this." The second is that this Sacrament commemorates the Lord's dying for our sake.

—*St. Albert*

PRAYER.   *St. Albert, when I receive the Holy Eucharist, remind me that Jesus lived, and died, and rose for us.*

NOV. 16   St. Margaret of Scotland +1093

I WILL walk in the path of blamelessness; when will You come to me? Within my house I will act with integrity of heart.   —Ps 101:2

REFLECTION.   When (Margaret) spoke, her words were seasoned with the salt of wisdom.

So fully did her disposition correspond with the soberness of her character that it was as if she bore the pattern of a virtuous life.   —*Turgot*

PRAYER.   *St. Margaret, you brought faith to your family and country. May my actions, increase the faith of my family and community.*

St. Elizabeth of Hungary +1231 NOV. 17

 ET your adornment be of your inner self, the imperishable beauty of a gentle and quiet spirit, which is precious in the sight of God. —1 Pet 3:4

REFLECTION. The world and all its joy is dead to me. —*St. Elizabeth, upon the death of her husband*

I heard a little bird singing. It sang so sweetly, I had to sing, too.

—*St. Elizabeth, at her death*

PRAYER. *St. Elizabeth, in 24 years you loved more fully than most who live to old age. Help me to be loving and generous.*

St. Rose Philippine Duchesne +1852 NOV. 18

HEN you grow old, you will stretch out your hands and someone else will put a belt around you and take you where you do not wish to go. —Jn 21:18

REFLECTION. We tend a very small field for Christ, but we do it with love, knowing that God does not require great things but a heart that holds back nothing.

The truest crosses are those we do not choose. . . . He who has Jesus has everything.

—*St. Rose*

PRAYER. *St. Rose, the Native Americans you served called you Woman-Who-Prays-Always. May I, too, pray always.*

NOV. 19   St. Obadiah +5th Century BC

THOSE who have been saved shall go up on Mount Zion . . . and the kingdom shall be the Lord's.   —Ob 21

REFLECTION.   For the day of the Lord is coming against all the nations. As you have done, it shall be done to you; your deeds shall return to you.   —St. Obadiah

PRAYER.   St. Obadiah, let me teach my community social justice by my own actions as much as by my words.

NOV. 20   St. Bernward +1022*

O if I, your Lord and Teacher, have washed your feet, you also should wash one another's feet.   —Jn 13:14

REFLECTION.   Remove irreverence and discord.

Calm violent and deadly disagreements that invade, divide, and disperse our communities. Let us aim at being good and generous.   —St. Lactantius

PRAYER.   St. Bernward, help me to conduct myself calmly, as you did, in the midst of disputes.

St. Gelasius +496*   NOV. 21

 ND I say to you: You are Peter, and on this rock I will build My Church.

—Mt 16:18

REFLECTION. No one at any time or under any pretext may proudly set himself above the office of him who by Christ's rule was set above everyone, and whom the universal Church has always recognized as its head.

—St. Gelasius

PRAYER. *St. Gelasius, you fought to free the Church from government interference. Free me from any allegiance that forms an obstacle between me and Jesus.*

St. Cecilia +Second Century   NOV. 22

 ING to God, sing praise to His name; exalt Him who rides upon the clouds.

—Ps 68:5

REFLECTION. Liturgical action is given a more noble form when sacred rites are solemnized in song, with the assistance of sacred ministers and the active participation of the people . . . so that . . . the voices of the people may ring out. —*Constitution on the Sacred Liturgy*

PRAYER. *St. Cecilia, patroness of musicians, remind me to lift my voice in songs of praise to the Almighty God.*

ND over all these put on love, which is the bond of perfection.   —Col 3:14

REFLECTION.   Grant us Lord, to set our hope on Your Name, the source of all creation.

We beg You, Lord and Master, to save those who are suffering; have mercy on the lowly; lift up the fallen.   —*St. Clement*

PRAYER.   *St. Clement, let me sow unity and love where there is strife and jealousy.*

AY all those who desire my ruin be . . . humiliated. May those who cry out to me, "Aha! Aha!" be forced to retreat.   —Ps 70:3-4

REFLECTION.   The Church in Vietnam is alive and vigorous, blessed with strong and faithful bishops, dedicated religious, and courageous and committed laypeople.

(It) is living out the gospel in a difficult and complex situation with remarkable persistence and strength.   —*U.S. Archbishops, 1989*

PRAYER.   *Sts. Andrew and Companions, thank you for bringing the word of God to the Vietnamese people.*

St. Catherine of Alexandria +Fourth Century

FOR the law of the Spirit of life in Christ Jesus has set you free from the law of sin and death. —Rom 8:2

REFLECTION. May my soul ever yearn for You; may my soul seek You, find You, always meditate on You, always speak of You, and do all things to the praise and glory of Your name.

You alone and forever are my hope.

—*St. Bonaventure*

PRAYER. *St. Catherine, help me to focus on Jesus with the same intensity as you did.*

St. Siricius +399*

NOV. 26

JESUS replied, "Unless I wash you, you will have no share with Me." —Jn 13:8

REFLECTION. Now the Lord Jesus, when He enlightened us by appearing, declared . . . that He had come to fulfill the law, not abolish it.

He desired that the Church . . . should shine with the splendor of chastity . . . in the Day of Judgment, when He comes again. —*St. Siricius*

PRAYER. *St. Siricius, I pray to Jesus to make me pure of heart, mind, and body.*

171

ACH of you is asserting, "I belong to Paul." . . . Has Christ now been divided? Did Paul die on the cross for you?

—1 Cor 1:12, 13

REFLECTION.   Never let anyone by your model for the tasks you have to do, however holy he may be.

Imitate Christ, Who is supremely perfect and supremely holy, and you will never err.

—*St. John of the Cross*

PRAYER.   *St. Virgil, you chose Christ even over men like St. Boniface. Help me to follow Jesus alone.*

NOV. 28   St. Stephen the Younger +764*

AY I never boast of anything except the cross of our Lord Jesus Christ, through which the world is crucified to me and I to the world.   —Gal 6:14

REFLECTION.   Look at Scripture with an ecclesiastical spirit and it will give you an image identical to the Church.

Contemplate Christ in and with His creation . . . and you will then stamp His image on your soul.   —*Johann Adam Mohler*

PRAYER.   *St. Stephen, you defended sacred images. Let my faith be increased and strengthened by sacred art and images.*

Bl. Dionysius and Bl. Redemptus +1638* — NOV. 29

THE words his mouth utters are malicious and deceitful; he has ceased to be wise and act uprightly. —Ps 36:4

REFLECTION. Believe that listening is always safer than talking, just as learning about God is better than teaching.

Worship a little with your words, but even more by your actions. —*St. Gregory Nazienzen*

PRAYER. *Bl. Dionysius and Bl. Redemptus, you remind me to use my skills to advance the cause of Christ.*

St. Andrew +First Century — NOV. 30

AS Jesus was walking by the Sea of Galilee, He saw two brothers, Simon who is called Peter and his brother, Andrew. —Mt 4:18

REFLECTION. Rabbi, where are You staying?
—*Andrew, upon meeting Jesus*

We have found the Messiah!
—*Andrew, telling Simon-Peter about Jesus*

PRAYER. *St. Andrew, you have the glorious name, Apostle! Help me to love Jesus as you did.*

DEC. 1   St. Nahum +Sixth Century BC.*

 ELEBRATE your festivals, O Judah, fulfill your vows, for never again shall the wicked invade you; they are utterly cut off.   —Nah 2:1

REFLECTION. The Lord is slow to anger, but abounds in power.

The Lord is good, a stronghold on a day of trouble; He protects those who take refuge in Him, even in a rushing flood.   —*St. Nahum*

PRAYER. *St. Nahum, as God's prophet, you spoke truths some didn't want to hear. Help me to listen to God's truth.*

DEC. 2 St. Chromatius of Aquileia +c. 407*

 OU are the light of the world. A city built upon a mountain cannot be hidden. Nor would someone light a lamp and then put it under a basket.   —Mt 5:14-15

REFLECTION. Since He is the Sun of Justice, He rightfully called His disciples the light of the world.

For by revealing the light of truth, they have dispelled the darkness of error from the hearts of men.   —*St. Chromatius*

PRAYER. *St. Chromatius, teach me to seek the shining light of Jesus in Scripture just as you did.*

St. Francis Xavier +1552   DEC. 3

OR He had healed so many that all who were afflicted in any way came crowding around to touch Him.   —Mk 3:10

REFLECTION. So great is the number of those who are being converted to Christ in this country . . . that often my arms are worn out from baptizing them.

Often I repeat the Creed and the commandments. Some days I baptize a whole village.

—*St. Francis*

PRAYER. *St. Francis, you inspire me to support foreign missions however I can: physically, prayerfully, financially.*

———————

St. John of Damascus +c. 749   DEC. 4

EANWHILE, encouraged by the Holy Spirit, the Church grew in numbers.   —Acts 9:31b

REFLECTION. And you, O Church, are an exceptional assembly, the noble summit of perfect integrity, whose help comes from God.

You, pious Christians, receive from us a statement of the Father that is free from error.

—*St. John*

PRAYER. *St. John, send us men and women from God who can clarify religious and civil teachings.*

DEC. 5   St. Crispina +304*

O not let me be put to shame, or permit my enemies to gloat over me. No one who places his hope in You will ever be put to shame. —Ps 25:2-3

REFLECTION. O God, Who was and is, You brought me to salvation through the waters of baptism. Be with me now and strengthen my soul that I will not weaken.

Praise to God Who has . . . delivered me from my enemies. —*St. Crispina*

PRAYER. *St. Crispina, you praised God as you were martyred. May I embrace God's plan for me.*

DEC. 6   St. Nicholas +c. 342

O not consider yourself to be better than others, but associate with the lowly, and never be conceited. —Rom 12:16

REFLECTION. In order to be able to consult . . . a bishop should strive to become duly acquainted with the needs of the faithful in the social circumstances in which they live.

He should manifest his concern for all.
—*Decree on the Pastoral Office of Bishops*

PRAYER. *St. Nicholas, caring bishop and generous benefactor, teach me compassion.*

OU, however, do not live according to the flesh but according to the Spirit since the Spirit of God dwells in you.

—Rom 8:9

REFLECTION.   All who are lead by the Spirit are children of God.

They are children of God because they did not receive a spirit of slavery, but the spirit of the children of adoption, so that the Holy Spirit bears witness with our spirit that we are children of God.   —*St. Ambrose*

PRAYER.   *St. Ambrose, help me follow where the Holy Spirit leads me, a child of God.*

Immaculate Conception   DEC. 8
of the Blessed Virgin Mary

OU brought Me out of the womb and made me feel secure upon My mother's breast.   —Ps 22:10

REFLECTION.   When I realize the eminence of God's grace in you, Mary, I find that you were placed not among but above all other creatures.

I conclude that in your conception you were not bound by the law of nature but . . . preserved from all taint of sin.

—*St. Eadmer of Canterbury*

PRAYER.   *Mary, I honor you for opening your womb and your heart to the Savior of the world.*

DEC. 9 St. Juan Diego +1548

ESUS . . . said to His mother, "Woman, behold, your Son." Then he said to the Disciple, "Behold, your mother." —Jn 19:26-27

REFLECTION. We could say that Juan Diego represents all the indigenous peoples who accepted the Gospel of Jesus, thanks to the maternal help of Mary, who is always connected to the manifestations of her Son and the spread of the Church. —*Pope John Paul II*

PRAYER. *St. Juan Diego, help me to willingly accept whatever Jesus and His mother call me to do.*

DEC. 10 St. Gregory III +741*

OVE the Lord, all His Saints. The Lord protects His loyal servants, but the arrogant He repays beyond measure. —Ps 31:24

REFLECTION. Let your baptism be your shield, your faith a helmet, your charity a spear, your patience a panoply.

Let your works be deposits, so that you may be repaid. In humility be patient . . . as God is with you. —*St. Ignatius of Antioch*

PRAYER. *St. Gregory, as Pope you were known for your humility. May people say the same of me.*

St. Damasus I +384   DEC. 11

N O one who places his hope in You will ever be put to shame, but shame will be the lot of all who break faith without justification. —Ps 25:3

REFLECTION. He who walking on the water could calm the bitter waves . . . He who was able to break the mortal chains of death, and after three nights could raise Lazarus: He, I believe, will make Damasus rise again from the dust. —*St. Damasus*

PRAYER. *St. Damasus, help me to rely on Jesus in times of trouble as you did.*

Our Lady of Guadalupe   DEC. 12

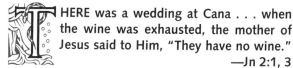

T HERE was a wedding at Cana . . . when the wine was exhausted, the mother of Jesus said to Him, "They have no wine." —Jn 2:1, 3

REFLECTION. My dearest son, I am the eternal Virgin Mary, Mother of the true God.

It is my desire that a church be built here . . . where, as your most merciful Mother, I may show my loving mercy and the compassion that I bear to the Indians.

—*Mary, appearing to Juan Diego*

PRAYER. *Mary, help me to rejoice in your compassion for all peoples of the world.*

DEC. 13   St. Lucy +c. 304/305

 HE eyes are the lamp of the body. If your eyes are sound, your whole body will be filled with light. —Mt 6:22

REFLECTION. Do not say that you have chaste minds if you have unchaste eyes, because an unchaste eye reveals an unchaste heart.

Lust served became a custom and custom not resisted became a necessity. —*St. Augustine*

PRAYER. *St. Lucy, give me the courage to keep my vows to Christ no matter how the world judges them, or me.*

DEC. 14   St. John of the Cross +1591

 OURS is royal dignity in the day of Your birth; in holy splendor, before the daystar, like the dew, I have begotten You.
—Ps 110:3

REFLECTION. Never was fount so clear,/ undimmed and bright;/ From it alone, I know proceeds all light,/ although 'tis night.

Whenever anything disagreeable happens to you, remember Christ crucified and be silent. —*St. John*

PRAYER. *St. John, open my eyes to the deeper, mystical meanings of God's Spirit in everything.*

St. Mary di Rosa +1855* DEC. 15

THEN he said, "Jesus, remember me when You come into Your kingdom."
—Lk 23:42

REFLECTION. And if He sees a thief hanging on the cross for his crime, He will bring him into Paradise through His goodness.

May all who love people be loving in their actions, as Christ was in His sufferings.
—*St. Gregory Nazianzen*

PRAYER. *St. Mary, when I think I've done enough for others, remind me that I'm just beginning.*

St. Haggai +c. Fifth Century BC* DEC. 16

IN the second year of King Darius, in the sixth month, on the first day of the month, the word of the Lord came by the prophet Haggai. —Hag 1:1

REFLECTION. Take courage all you people of the land, says the Lord; work, for I am with you, says the Lord of hosts, according to the promise that I made you when you came out of Egypt.

My spirit lives in you; do not fear. —*Haggai*

PRAYER. *St. Haggai, give me the skill to speak to others as the Lord instructs me.*

DEC. 17 — St. John of Matha +1213*

H E was separated from you for awhile so that you might have him back forever, no longer as a slave, but . . . as a brother.
—Philem 15-16

REFLECTION. I felt like a slave freed from prison and chains to enter the house of her beloved . . . to rejoice, absolutely free, in His presence, His riches, His love.
—St. Margaret Mary Alacoque

PRAYER. St. John, you risked everything to free slaves. My I be free from bondage to sin so that I can better free others.

DEC. 18 — St. Malachi +c. Fourth/Fifth Century BC*

S EE I am sending My messenger to prepare the way before Me, and the Lord whom you seek will suddenly come to His temple.
—Mal 3:1

REFLECTION. Have we not all one Father? Has not one God created us?

Whey then are we faithless to one another, blaspheming the covenant of our ancestors?
—St. Malachi

PRAYER. St. Malachi, you prophesied the coming of Jesus, heralded by John the Baptist. Teach me to prepare the way of the Lord in my world.

Bl. Urban V +1370*   DEC. 19

ATHER his delight is in the law of the Lord, and on that law he meditates day and night.   —Ps 1:2

REFLECTION.   Read unceasingly the precepts of the Lord and you will know what to avoid and what to pursue.

Without discretion virtue becomes vice and the natural impulses serve only to upset and destroy the personality.   —St. Bernard

PRAYER.   *Bl. Urban, you were a prudent Pope who supported education. Help me to seek knowledge and wisdom in the Lord.*

St. Dominic of Silos +1073*   DEC. 20

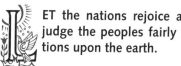

ET the nations rejoice and exult, for You judge the peoples fairly and guide the nations upon the earth.   —Ps 67:5

REFLECTION.   You are a fire that burns away the chill, illuminates the mind with its light, and helps me to know You are beauty and wisdom itself.

The food of Angels, You give yourself to man in the fire of Your love.   —St. Catherine of Siena

PRAYER.   *St. Dominic, you reserved yourself for God. Help me to be on fire with my love for the Lord.*

St. Peter Canisius +1597

 HE water that I will give him will become a spring of water within him welling up to eternal life. —Jn 4:14

REFLECTION. It was as if You opened to me the heart of Your most sacred body. I seemed to see it right before my eyes.

You told me to drink from this fountain, inviting me, to draw the waters of my salvation from Your wellsprings, my Savior.

—St. Peter

PRAYER. *St. Peter, like I seek the waters of everlasting life in Jesus.*

St. Chaeremon +250*

 SERVANT of the Lord should not engage in quarrels but should be kind to everyone. —2 Tim 2:24

REFLECTION. O God the Father: Origin of Divinity, Good beyond all that is good, Fair beyond all that is fair, in whom is calmness, peace, concord:

Heal the disagreements that divide us . . . and restore us to the unity of love that matches Your divine nature. —St. Dionysius

PRAYER. *St. Chaeremon, mourned by Dionysius, let me turn my disturbances over to God and embrace His peace.*

St. John of Kanty +1473   DEC. 23

OVE is patient; love is charitable. Love is not envious . . . it is not filled with its own importance. —1 Cor 13:4

REFLECTION. God does not want you to be sad. If I have done any good for you all these years, sing a song of joy.

Contest all false opinions, but let your weapons be patience, sweetness, and love.

—*St. John*

PRAYER. *St. John, let my weapons be patience, sweetness, and love.*

All the Holy Ancestors   DEC. 24
of Jesus Christ

HEN God said to Noah . . . "I am establishing My Covenant with you and your descendants after you." —Gen 9:8

REFLECTION. Do not press me to leave you!

Where you go, I will go; where you lodge, I will lodge; your people shall be my people, and your God, my God. —*St. Ruth*

PRAYER. *Holy Ancestors of Jesus Christ, show me the way to know and follow my Savior and Lord, Jesus Christ.*

DEC. 25   **The Nativity of our Lord and Savior Jesus Christ**

OR this day in the city of David there has been born to you a Savior who is Christ, the Lord. —Lk 2:11

REFLECTION. Dearly Beloved, today our Savior is born; let us rejoice. Sadness has no place on the birthday of life.

The fear of death has been swallowed up; life brings us joy with the promise of eternal happiness. —St. Leo the Great

PRAYER. *I dedicate my life to Jesus, who came into the world as a helpless Babe and left it as Messiah.*

DEC. 26   **St. Stephen** +35

TEPHEN, filled with grace and power, began to work great wonders and signs among the people. —Acts 6:8

REFLECTION. Look, I see the heavens opened and the Son of Man standing at the right hand of God!

Lord Jesus, receive my spirit. Lord, do not hold this sin against them. —St. Stephen

PRAYER. *St. Stephen, first martyr for Christ, give me the courage to proclaim the Lord Jesus Christ as Savior, even when I risk rejection or persecution.*

St. John +c. 100 — DEC. 27

THEN the other disciple, the one who had reached the tomb first, also went inside and he saw and believed. —Jn 20:8

REFLECTION. The way we came to know love was that He lay down His life for us; so we ought to lay down our lives for our brothers.

God is love, and whoever remains in love remains in God and God in him. —*St. John*

PRAYER. *St. John, help me to devote my whole life to becoming worthy to be, with you, a disciple whom the Lord loves.*

———————

The Holy Innocents — DEC. 28

A VOICE was heard in Ramah, sobbing and loud lamentations; Rachel weeping for her children. —Mt 2:18

REFLECTION. The children die for Christ, though they do not know it. The parents mourn for the death of martyrs.

The Christ child makes of those as yet unable to speak fit witnesses to Himself. But you, Herod, do not know this. —*St. Quodvuldeus*

PRAYER. *Holy Innocents, protect all children who are the victims of fear, hatred, and cruelty.*

DEC. 29   St. Thomas Becket +1170

 ETER answered, "Repent and be baptized . . . in the name of Jesus Christ so that your sins may be forgiven, and you will receive the gift of the Holy Spirit." —Acts 2:37-38

REFLECTION. The Church of Rome remains the highest of all churches and the source of Catholic teaching. Of this there can be no doubt.

Everyone knows that the keys of the kingdom of heaven were given to Peter. —*St. Thomas*

PRAYER. *St. Thomas, I pray for all leaders of the Church and the world to seek God's guidance.*

DEC. 30   St. Anysius +c. 406*

 LESSED are the people who know how to acclaim You, O Lord, who walk in the light of Your countenance. —Ps 89:16

REFLECTION. Prayer and conversation with God is an extreme good. It is a relationship and union with God.

Prayer is the light of the spirit, true knowledge of God, mediating between God and man. Prayer stands before God as an honored ambassador. —*St. John Chrysostom*

PRAYER. *St. Anysius, praised and thanked by your contemporaries like St. John Chrysostom, lead me to Christian companions.*

St. Catherine Labouré +1876 DEC. 31

 DAY after day, I was with you in the temple teaching . .. . but let the Scriptures be fulfilled. —Mk 14:49

REFLECTION. Whenever I go to the chapel, I put myself in the Presence of our good Lord, and I say to Him, "Lord, I am here. Tell me what You (would) have me do."

—*St. Catherine Labouré*

PRAYER. *St. Catherine, open my eyes, ears and heart to whatever messages Mary and her Blessed Son might have for me in the coming year and always.*

Litany of the Saints

LORD, have mercy.
Lord, have mercy.

Christ, have mercy.
Christ, have mercy.

Lord, have mercy.
Lord, have mercy.

Holy Mary, Mother of God, *pray for us.*

Saint Michael, *pray for us.*

Holy angels of God, *pray for us.*

Saint John the Baptist, *pray for us.*

Saint Joseph, *pray for us.*

Saint Peter and Saint Paul, *pray for us.*

Saint Andrew, *pray for us.*

Saint John, *pray for us.*

Saint Mary Magdalene, *pray for us.*

Saint Stephen, *pray for us.*

Saint Ignatius, *pray for us.*

Saint Lawrence, *pray for us.*

Saint Perpetua and Saint Felicity, *pray for us.*

Saint Agnes, *pray for us.*

Saint Gregory, *pray for us.*

Saint Augustine, *pray for us.*

Saint Athanasius, *pray for us.*

Saint Basil, *pray for us.*

Saint Martin, *pray for us.*

Saint Benedict, *pray for us.*

Saint Francis and Saint Dominic, *pray for us.*

Saint Francis Xavier, *pray for us.*

Saint John Vianney, *pray for us.*

Saint Catherine, *pray for us.*

Saint Teresa, *pray for us.*

All holy men and women, *pray for us.*

Lord, be merciful, *Lord, save your people.*

From all evil, *Lord, save your people.*

From every sin, *Lord, save your people.*

From everlasting death, *Lord, save your people.*

By your coming as man, *Lord, save your people.*

By your death and rising to new life, *Lord, save your people.*

By your gift of the Holy Spirit, *Lord, save your people.*

Be merciful to us sinners, *Lord, hear our prayer.*

Give new life to these chosen ones by the grace of baptism, *Lord, hear our prayer.*

Jesus, Son of the living God, *Lord, hear our prayer.*

Christ, hear us.

Christ, hear us.

Lord Jesus, hear our prayer.

Lord Jesus, hear our prayer.

The Saints in Our Lives

WHEN we look at the lives of the Saints,
those who have faithfully followed Christ,
we are inspired with a new reason for seeking
heaven
and at the same time we are shown a most safe
path
by which in keeping with our state of life on
earth
we will be able to arrive at perfect union with
Christ.

In the lives of those who,
sharing our humanity,
are however more perfectly transformed
into the image of Christ,
God vividly manifests His presence and His
face
to human beings.
He speaks to us in them
and gives us a sign of His Kingdom,
to which we are strongly drawn.

The authentic devotion to the Saints consists
not so much in the multiplication of external
acts
but rather in greater intensity of our love. . . .
We seek from the Saints
example in their way of life,
fellowship in their communion,
and aid in their intercession.

Vatican Council II: *Constitution on the Church*, no. 50

OTHER OUTSTANDING CATHOLIC BOOKS

AUGUSTINE ON PRAYER—An excellent summary of the great African Bishop's teaching on prayer in the life of Christians. Over 500 Augustinian texts. **Ask for No. 171**

SAINT AUGUSTINE: Man, Pastor, Mystic—By Rev. Augustine Trapé, O.S.A. A masterful biography of one of the greatest Saints in the Church by a world-renowned scholar. Large type and magnificently illustrated. **Ask for No. 172**

CONFESSIONS OF ST. AUGUSTINE—New translation of the Christian classic that—after the Bible and the Imitation of Christ—is the most widely translated and the most universally esteemed. It is published in prayerbook format as befits its nature.. **Ask for No. 173**

WORDS OF COMFORT FOR EVERY DAY—Short meditation for every day including a Scripture text and a meditative prayer to God the Father. Printed in two colors. 192 pages. **Ask for No. 186**

MARY DAY BY DAY—Minute meditations for every day of the year, including a Scripture passage, a quotation from the Saints, and a concluding prayer. Printed in two colors with over 300 illustrations. **Ask for No. 180**

MINUTE MEDITATIONS FROM THE POPES—By Rev. Jude Winkler, O.F.M. Conv. Minute meditations for every day of the year using the words of twentieth-century Popes. Printed and illustrated in two colors. **Ask for No. 175**

BIBLE DAY BY DAY—By Rev. John Kersten, S.V.D. Minute Bible meditations for every day including a short Scripture text and brief reflection. Printed in two colors with 300 illustrations. **Ask for No. 150**

LIVING WISDOM FOR EVERY DAY—By Rev. Bennet Kelley, C.P. Choice texts from St. Paul of the Cross, one of the true Masters of Spirituality, and a prayer for each day. **Ask for No. 182**

MINUTE MEDITATIONS FOR EACH DAY— By Rev. Bede Naegele O.C.D. This very attractive book offers a short Scripture text, a practical reflection, and a meaningful prayer for each day of the year. **Ask for No. 190**

WHEREVER CATHOLIC BOOKS ARE SOLD

ISBN 978-0-89942-183-4

90000